# *Celebrating* EASTER

THE 2006 BYU EASTER CONFERENCE

THE 2006 BYU EASTER CONFERENCE

# Celebrating EASTER

*Edited by*
THOMAS A. WAYMENT
*and*
KEITH J. WILSON

FOREWORD BY
RICHARD NEITZEL HOLZAPFEL
AND THOMAS A. WAYMENT

RELIGIOUS STUDIES CENTER
BRIGHAM YOUNG UNIVERSITY

Front cover: The Garden Tomb, Jerusalem. Used by permission, Z. Radovan/BibleLandPictures.com. Most scholars, including several Latter-day Saint specialists, have found evidence to suggest that the Garden Tomb may not be the exact location of the Savior's burial. However, the actual burial place may be within a few hundred feet of this location. Nevertheless, the peaceful garden, empty tomb, and reverent spirit here conform to the expectations of those who seek a reverent place to pray, read, and ponder New Testament passages describing Jesus's death, burial, and Resurrection.

Frontispiece: Carl Bloch, *Doubting Thomas*. Courtesy of Brigham Young University Museum of Art. All rights reserved.

Published by the Religious Studies Center, Brigham Young University, Provo, Utah

© 2007 by Brigham Young University
All rights reserved

Any uses of this material beyond those allowed by the exemptions in U.S. copyright law, such as section 107, "Fair Use," and section 108, "Library Copying," require the written permission of the publisher, Religious Studies Center, 167 HGB, Brigham Young University, Provo, Utah 84602. The views expressed herein are the responsibility of the authors and do not necessarily represent the position of Brigham Young University or the Religious Studies Center.

ISBN 978-0-8425-2669-2

# Contents

**FOREWORD**
*Richard Neitzel Holzapfel and Thomas A. Wayment*    vii

1. **TESTIMONY OF JESUS CHRIST**
   *President Cecil O. Samuelson*    1

2. **CHRIST, OUR ADVOCATE AND HIGH PRIEST**
   *John S. Tanner*    19

3. **THE UNIQUE AND SUPREME ATTRIBUTES OF JESUS THE CHRIST**
   *Terry B. Ball*    33

4. **THE DILEMMA: AN INCOMPREHENSIBLE ATONEMENT?**
   *Russell C. Rasmussen*    43

5. **JESUS, THE GREAT SHEPHERD-KING**
   *Dana M. Pike*    61

6. THE BREAD OF LIFE SERMON
*Eric D. Huntsman*     87

7. JESUS CHRIST:
THE SAVIOR WHO KNOWS
*Frank F. Judd Jr.*     113

8. HOSTILITY TOWARD JESUS:
PRELUDE TO THE PASSION
*Jennifer C. Lane*     137

9. THE LEGAL CAUSE OF ACTION
AGAINST JESUS IN JOHN 18:29–30
*John W. Welch*     157

10. "IT IS FINISHED": THE DIVINE
ACCOMPLISHMENT OF THE CRUCIFIXION
*Richard E. Bennett*     177

11. THE CHRISTIAN HISTORY
AND DEVELOPMENT OF EASTER
*Keith J. Wilson*     201

12. TEACHING THE DOCTRINE
OF THE RESURRECTION
WHEN SHARING THE GOSPEL
*Rick B. Jorgensen*     225

INDEX
*245*

# Foreword

O f all the events in the Savior's life—His birth, baptism, death, and Resurrection—early Christians likely celebrated the day of the Resurrection before anything else. This celebration was first carried out on a weekly basis, as reflected in the shift from Saturday worship services (the Jewish practice) to Sunday meetings (the Christian practice). Even before the early church officially changed to meeting on Sunday to commemorate the Resurrection, there was likely some recognition of the importance of Sunday.

As time progressed and early Christians began meeting every Sunday, they also began to celebrate and remember the actual day on which Jesus Christ was resurrected—the first Sunday of the Passover feast. Initially this celebration was closely linked with the date of the Jewish Passover, falling on the first Sunday of Passover, but in later decades as the Christian Church became more formally distinct from Judaism, Christians began celebrating the Resurrection of Christ according to their own calendrical calculations.

They remembered that Jesus was crucified on the eve of Passover, but because of certain peculiarities with the way the Jews managed their calendar, Christians felt that at times the celebration of the day of Jesus's Resurrection might be off by several weeks. Therefore, they were careful to determine each year through episcopal and later papal decree—sometimes referred to as a festal letter—the exact date of the celebration of Christ's Resurrection. It was so important to determine the correct date, in fact, that a sect of Christians known as the Quartodecimans were declared heretics by the orthodox church because they celebrated the Resurrection on a different day.

Initially this annual celebration was not named Easter. Christians in the East and West referred to the celebration using the term *Pascha*, derived from the Greek *to pascha* and the Hebrew term for Passover (*pesah*), a tradition that continues to this day (e.g. Latin, *Paschalia*; Italian, *Pasqua*; Dutch, *Paschen*). But beginning in the early Middle Ages, Christians in England began referring to the event under a new designation—Easter. In reality, only English speakers refer to the celebration of Christ's Resurrection using the term *Easter* (though it is related to the German *Ostem*), a word that many feel has a pagan origin. The link between the earliest celebration associated directly with Passover and the modern celebration of Easter is often more evident in other societies, where the modern word still clearly reflects the Passover of Christ's Resurrection.

## Foreword

It is safe to say without equivocation that the Resurrection of Christ, which signaled to all humankind that the Atonement was complete, is the most important event in the salvation of men and women and the cosmos itself. That is not to say, however, that the celebration of the event has always received sufficient attention. For a variety of reasons, Christmas and the attendant celebration of Christ's birth have received the most attention in the modern era even though the celebration of His birthday was a significantly later development. Ironically, it was not Christ's birth that saved us but His suffering, death, and Resurrection. If there had been no suffering and death, there would have been no forgiveness of sin. If there had been no empty tomb, there would have been no triumph over death, and therefore no Christianity.

Easter celebrations in other denominations take on a variety of forms. Some celebrate the entire Passion Week (the final week of Jesus's life), which includes recognition of important events from that week: the Triumphal Entry (Palm Sunday), the Last Supper (Maundy Thursday), the Crucifixion (Good Friday), and the Resurrection (Easter Sunday). Other denominations begin the celebrations in February to celebrate Shrove Tuesday—the day before Ash Wednesday, when Lent begins—while some extend the celebration into May when they celebrate Pentecost, which occurs fifty days after Easter. For those unfamiliar with them, these celebrations may seem foreign even though each of them has a strong biblical precedent. The issue is even more pronounced in the western United States, where Good Friday is not typically observed as a public holiday.

Celebrating Easter

Many Christians attempt to extend the celebration of Easter in recognition of the importance of that day.

Though Latter-day Saints have not traditionally celebrated all of the events typically associated with Easter, these events are an important focus of the talks given in the spring general conference. Moreover, Latter-day Saints recognize the comparatively greater importance of the Resurrection of Christ in comparison to His birth even if their outward celebration of those two holidays does not reflect those sentiments. Easter will always have profound meaning for Latter-day Saints, and while we may never officially observe all of the events associated with the final week of His life as other Christians do, we join with them in celebrating the crowning achievement of that week—the Resurrection.

In 2003, the Brigham Young University faculty held its first conference on the life of Jesus Christ in an attempt to gather thoughts on the meaning of His life for us both as Latter-day Saints and as participants of a wider world. In conjunction with the conference, we published a book of collected articles focusing on the Savior's final hours. After years of training and research, we hoped to be able to enter into the important academic discussion of Christ's life with fresh insights and with the most recent archeological and textual discoveries. We stood on the shoulders of great men and women of our faith who had made this discussion possible, many of whom passed away before the Dead Sea Scrolls, the Nag Hammadi Codices, and other important discoveries had come to light. We wanted to renew their work again in our own day, adding to the discussion the knowledge of our time.

## Foreword

The first volume and the associated conference, which we held at BYU's Salt Lake City extension center, were delightful successes, and many responded with positive notes and encouragement, some even suggesting that we should consider Jesus's entire life anew. So we pressed forward in order to produce two more volumes on the life of Jesus, effectively covering His life from birth and to His final week to His Resurrection. The first book was republished as the third volume in the series; we entitled the whole *The Life and Teachings of Jesus Christ*.

Because of the overwhelmingly positive response and the need we had for larger facilities, we moved the conference to Provo to accommodate the growing crowds. The second conference was held in 2005 in conjunction with the publication of the second volume in the series. Again, the conference was an overwhelming success, and many offered words of encouragement and interest in the topics we had discussed. We realized at that time that there was a great interest in both the Easter season and in the possibility of meeting each year at that time to discuss the life of Jesus. We redoubled our efforts and produced the final volume in time to hold a third conference the following year, 2006, in conjunction with the publication of the last volume in the series.

But it occurred to us that holding the conference on Easter weekend also demanded that we speak of the Resurrection even though the publication that the conference celebrated discussed a wide variety of other important topics. Therefore, instead of focusing only on the topics we had published, we changed the focus to

Easter and the Resurrection of Jesus Christ and planned to host an annual Easter conference at BYU.

This new conference would provide many opportunities for us to discuss the meaning of the Atonement and Resurrection of Jesus Christ in conjunction with our celebration of the days on which those events occurred historically. It was therefore unique in its scope and purpose because it would allow us to reflect on Jesus's life at precisely the time of year when He offered His life as a sacrifice for us.

As the discussion of the importance of Easter began to take shape in our minds, we realized that the conference might help us begin to formulate our own unique approach to this important holiday. We invited talented speakers and scholars, giving each the opportunity to reflect specifically on Easter. We intentionally did not provide the presenters with their subjects; instead we wanted to see the direction they would take given the broad scope of the conference, named "The Brigham Young University 2006 Easter Conference." In fact, we attempted to perform a study within a study—while the presenters studied Easter, we studied how a group of gifted and talented scholars approached this issue.

This volume is a collection of essays from the conference and reflects some of the ways in which we think about Easter. The presentations ranged from direct studies about how Latter-day Saints celebrate and teach Easter to technical aspects of the Savior's trial and His Jewish antagonists' approach to His miracles. In all, we realize that Easter is vitally important in our thinking and in our discussions of Jesus's life, but for the most part,

## Foreword

when it comes to speaking about Easter directly, we tend to discuss the details of Jesus's life and ministry rather than the meaning of the Easter message directly.

The reasons for doing so are not negative. In reality, many prophets and apostles both modern and ancient have testified about the meaning of the Resurrection in our worship services. Further consideration on this topic may appear to some, therefore, to be unnecessary given the clear prophetic council on the subject. Pushing further in our scholarship on the subject may put us in the uncomfortable position of going beyond the revealed word of prophets and apostles. On the other hand, our outward celebration of Easter does not reflect our recognition of the importance of the event. So how do we as Latter-day Saints bring these two aspects of Easter into greater harmony?

One of the profound truths in this volume may be the simple fact that it does reflect the unique Latter-day Saint position on the subject: the Resurrection clearly announces that Jesus lives, that He has conquered death, and that He has authored our salvation. His life looks forward, but His death thrusts us back into His mortal life before He atoned for us. One of the uniquely Latter-day Saint views on the subject is that in commemorating the event we focus on new life and celebrate the continuing life of Christ. In other words, living the gospel in the present is a tribute to the true meaning and purpose of Easter. Further discussions may reveal whether that has been an intentional choice or whether it was achieved through default.

Whether we will ever recognize the traditional Christian calendar of events associated with Easter or whether we will ever even become familiar with its terminology is a poignant issue. However, the doctrine of Easter still permeates our thinking and scholarship. Some of the most recognized verses in all of modern canon reflect the triumph of Easter: "And now, after the many testimonies which have been given of him, this is the testimony, last of all, which we give of him: That he lives!" (D&C 76:22).

Richard Neitzel Holzapfel<br>Thomas A. Wayment

PRESIDENT CECIL O. SAMUELSON

# Testimony of Jesus Christ

These Easter conferences have been wonderful, and today's is no exception. After accepting the invitation to speak, I began to think earnestly about what I might contribute to this remarkable program. As I reviewed the outstanding list of faculty and topics for today's conference and those of previous years, I concluded that my participation likely could not add much, with the possible exception of one consideration. I hope I might assist in our quest today by fulfilling my responsibility as a witness of the reality of the Resurrection and all events associated with it.

As you know, my calling as a Seventy is to "preach the gospel" and to be a witness of Jesus Christ (see D&C 107:25). While my scholarship, such as it is, is largely in

---

President Cecil O. Samuelson is a member of the First Quorum of the Seventy and president of Brigham Young University.

arenas far from the expertise of our speakers and the topics of today's presentations, my testimony is not distanced from them and is, I believe, germane to the Easter season.

In this regard, I would like to begin by relating some autobiographical learning events that have affected me significantly and seem appropriate to share. I shall not dwell on details, nor shall I mention other profound personal and sacred experiences that are vital to my having a firm testimony and an unreserved witness of the Lord Jesus Christ. Let me just assure you that what I know, I know clearly and more reliably than the many things that I have learned or understood through traditional study, experimentation in the laboratory, and life experiences.

I confess that I have always had a testimony of Jesus Christ and His mission. I have wondered about many things, but the reality of the Savior has never been one of those. The Brethren used to talk about believing blood more than they do today. Having been something of a geneticist for a period of my academic career, I believe that I largely inherited my believing blood, together with growing up in a supportive environment, and am grateful for that heritage, which has made much of my life so much easier.

As I have tried to analyze my testimony and what has strengthened it, I have concluded that study, faith, and obedience are critical to obtaining and sustaining a testimony, but there is something more. Let me attempt to explain what I mean by relating some personal experiences.

The first occurred some thirty years ago. By then, I was a returned missionary and had had several Church

## "Testimony of Jesus Christ"

leadership experiences. I was young, but I was not really a rookie. As a stake president, I had chosen to speak about spiritual gifts in a stake conference because some questions had arisen on this topic among a few members of our stake. While I was speaking, I read these verses from the forty-sixth section of the Doctrine and Covenants: "For all have not every gift given unto them; for there are many gifts, and to every man is given a gift by the Spirit of God. To some is given one, and to some is given another, that all may be profited thereby. To some it is given by the Holy Ghost to know that Jesus Christ is the Son of God, and that he was crucified for the sins of the world" (vv. 11–13).

As I read that last verse, "To some it is given by the Holy Ghost to know that Jesus Christ is the Son of God, and that he was crucified for the sins of the world," it came to me, with greater power than I had ever experienced, that I had been given that gift. It was not that I had not previously had a conviction about Jesus Christ and His unique and supernal role, because I had, as I have mentioned. It was the dramatic realization, confirmed by the Holy Ghost, that I indeed had this specific gift, which is not the routine possession of everyone else. I have never forgotten that moment.

The second experience followed just months after the first. My wife, Sharon, and I, with some good friends, had the privilege of going to Israel. We had a great time and visited most of the special and expected sites throughout the Holy Land. When we visited the Garden Tomb, we were not alone and, in fact, found ourselves in a long line waiting for our turn to look into the burial vault.

Our guide and the caretaker at the tomb was a retired British army colonel who was tall, slender, and ramrod-straight in his demeanor. He was serving as a missionary for another denomination from England and clearly was a committed Christian with a well-developed sense of propriety and reverence. He asked for people to be respectful of this sacred site and to keep voices low because there were those in the area praying and meditating.

Just ahead of us in the line were a couple of American women with accents that made me think they were from a borough in our largest American city. They loudly commented about how much time the line was taking and how it was interfering with their planned shopping. The guide said nothing to them directly but was clearly a little irritated by them, and we were embarrassed by our fellow countrywomen. Their dialogue continued almost nonstop until they finally reached the opening of the tomb. The first one there said, "Why, Ethel, there is nothing in here!" Our wonderful British caretaker said with admirable restraint, "Madam, that is precisely the point!" My witness of the reality of the Resurrection was again clearly, but quietly and personally, confirmed for me that day.

Many, including those of other Christian faiths, believe in the Resurrection and the divinity of Jesus Christ. However, it is a special blessing to know that He is the Christ, the Savior and the Redeemer, and that He lives today.

The third experience I will relate occurred in the fall of 1997. I was serving as the Europe North Area President and living in England. One day I received a very nice letter from the Divinity School at the University of Nottingham inviting me to participate in a seminar series on "alternative religions." In an evening session each month, this group of clerics and graduate students in the ministry would invite a leader from another religious tradition to spend two hours with them. The format they suggested was that I might say anything I wished for the first half hour, and then the remaining hour and a half would be devoted to a question-and-answer session both on what was said and what they had previously read or wondered about. In other words, it would be open season!

My first inclination, candidly, was to think of whom else I might send to respond to this invitation. I add parenthetically that for a number of years, Nottingham University had been quite friendly to Latter-day Saints. Professor Douglas Davies had, until just a year or two before, been at Nottingham, and several of our British Church Educational System personnel had obtained graduate degrees in his program. By then, he had moved north to Durham University. For all the obvious reasons, I felt that I needed to respond and appear.

Accordingly, I arrived at the appointed time and place on campus and was treated quite graciously. As I entered the modest classroom, quite bleak by BYU standards, I noted that several of the approximately forty in attendance had missionary copies of the Book of Mormon on their desks with their Bibles and other papers. Several of the copies of the Book of Mormon had little yellow Post-it notes marking selected pages and passages. I sensed I was in for some serious discussion. I also had my scriptures, but my Bible was different from theirs. All that I saw on their tables were fairly recent revision or translation editions, and mine was the only King James Version I could see.

You can imagine much of what transpired. I took the first thirty minutes in telling them a little of our history, beginning with the First Vision, the visitations of the angel Moroni, the restoration of the priesthood, the translation of the Book of Mormon, the organization of the Church, and, briefly, our Church history in Great Britain. They listened courteously, most took some notes and all waited patiently for the question-and-answer period. Virtually all seemed to know something about us, and I sensed they were serious in their desire to understand.

Their initial questions were kind and respectful and related to such things as their wonderment that my professional training was not in religion or theology, given my Church leadership assignment; that Latter-day Saints were so willing to respond to mission calls; and that we had really abandoned plural marriage—or had we?

Soon we got into doctrinal matters that focused on Latter-day Saint beliefs in continuing revelation, an open canon of scripture, a lay priesthood, and similar matters. We also discussed why Latter-day Saints do not accept the creeds and councils of other traditions and why we also believe an apostasy took place.

Several had marked the Book of Mormon passages that suggest that the Father, Son, and Holy Ghost are "one God." They read to me the words of Abinadi in chapter 15 of Mosiah and wondered aloud if Abinadi did not actually believe in the Catholic Trinity. We talked of the Savior's great Intercessory Prayer recorded in John 17 and other clarifying passages. It was clear that they thought my interpretation was quaint, but one opined that he could understand my confusion. We do not have time today to relate all of their questions in detail, but the discourse and our discussion were respectful, cordial, and rather wide ranging.

Then in the last half hour, we finally got to the question that I should have been expecting. It went something like this: In light of the many differences you and we have identified between your beliefs and ours, how do you justify calling yourselves Christians?

Because I had been so conditioned in our Latter-day Saint culture, I honestly thought that I had already spent an hour explaining our belief in Jesus Christ and His centrality to our theology and religious practice. At the moment of my growing frustration, I was helped by heaven in a way that had not occurred to me previously. I felt a spirit of calmness and comfort as a response to them formed within me.

I had already mentioned to the group my high regard for the King James Version and my appreciation for the role of England and its courageous reformers who made the Bible readily available to all of us. We had discussed our divergent views on the current utility of the King James Version and also the Joseph Smith Translation, which they described as curious.

Wanting to avoid any of these issues or distractions in my response to their central question, I asked our discussion leader if I might borrow his Bible to use in answering my question. He readily handed it to me. I then asked the group if I might answer the question posed to me by asking them a few brief questions first. They nodded in agreement.

I lifted a red-covered International Translation and, without opening it, asked if they accepted it as the word of God. Again, they nodded in assent.

I then asked three questions, asking them to answer only to themselves unless they wished to vocalize a response. The first was, "Do you accept your Bible's version of the origins of Jesus Christ?" Some looked a little puzzled, and so I amplified by asking, "Do you believe that He was literally the physical Son of God the Father and Mary, a mortal mother?" Some nodded yes, some looked down, and some looked pained. I then told them that we, as Latter-day Saints, accept this biblical teaching without reservation.

The second question was, "Do you accept your Bible's account of Jesus's mortal ministry? This includes the miracles that He performed and the organization of His Church with Apostles having His authority to minister and administrate." Again, I noticed the same general spectrum of mute responses as with the first question. As with the first query, my answer was the same: we accept the biblical account without qualification. We then had a brief aside on the Lord's miracles, and several admitted to being unsettled as to their literal veracity.

The third question was then presented: "Do you accept your Bible's account of Christ's Passion [to use a term more familiar to them than to us], His experience in the Garden of Gethsemane, His Crucifixion on Golgotha, and His literal Resurrection on the third day?" A few remained passive, but several of the group now needed to speak. Interestingly, the most agitated wanted to talk about the Resurrection as being only symbolic of new life such as in the spring when the flowers and trees come out and blossom.

It was obvious that many were troubled by the thought of a literal resurrection, and a couple of them even expressed doubts about individual life after death. After a few minutes of various opinions, I replied that we as Latter-day Saints fully accept the biblical account of the Resurrection of Jesus.

I further bore my testimony of its truthfulness and then asked my last question. "Given the answers to the questions I have just posed, who do you think deserves to be called Christian?" Again, there were various looks and no comments except from one graduate student who elbowed the previously vocal fellow next to her who had asked the question concerning our Christianity and said, "It looks like he got you there."

The time was up, and the moderator took back the floor with gracious expressions of thanks and best wishes. Several of the attendees made civil and generous comments, although I am not aware that anyone's previous convictions were altered. Three or four of the group lingered for a few minutes longer and expressed appreciation for our evening together as they had not understood how strongly we feel about the Savior. I do not tell this experience to be critical nor to make light of the feelings and beliefs of these good people. I believe that they were doing the best they could with the understanding that was theirs. I left them with increased appreciation for their general goodness. I also felt increased gratitude for the Holy Ghost and for my sustaining testimony of the Savior.

Two of them accepted my invitation to attend the open house for the new Preston England Temple, then under construction. At the visit to the temple open house, both of these new friends went out of their way to mention the clear evidence they saw in the artwork and other materials of our strong feelings about Jesus Christ.

I have not been invited to any of their baptisms into the restored Church, nor do I think that this has occurred. I do believe that what was most impressive and surprising to them about us and our theology is our testimony of the Savior.

Just last Sunday, I was introduced to an investigator who had come to the general session of stake conference where I was assigned. As we visited briefly, she asked if I was going to talk about Palm Sunday, it being Palm Sunday. I responded and told her I indeed planned to speak about the Savior and some of the events related to His Atonement, Crucifixion, and Resurrection. She seemed somewhat relieved and reported that someone had told her that we do not worship the same Jesus others do. I told her that we worship the Living Christ and that she would hear several testimonies in music and talks that would demonstrate our convictions about and reverence for Him. That turned out to be the case, and I was grateful that it was so.

It did remind me of an experience of almost eight years ago. At that time, we were holding the open-house tours for the recently completed Preston England Temple immediately prior to the dedication services scheduled for a couple of weeks hence. One of our tour supervisors approached me with some anxiety and said that a known critic and antagonist of the Church was in one of the tour groups and that the guide of that group was a fine man but also a fairly recent convert with limited speaking and leadership experience. The plea to me was to go with the group and rescue him. Accordingly, I found the group and lingered near the back where I could observe all that transpired and hopefully render some assistance to our guide if necessary.

It was not long before the outspoken opponent tried to take over the tour. Our guide was doing a fine job and was explaining the centrality of Jesus Christ to our theology. The critic interrupted and said something like, "How do you claim to be Christians and you don't even celebrate Holy Week?" Happily, I restrained myself and just listened. Our sweet guide, seemingly unruffled, just said, "Why sir, *every week* for us is Holy Week. Each Sabbath day we meet to partake of the sacred emblems of the sacrament, where we promise to always remember Him, to keep His commandments, and plead to always have His Spirit to be with us." I thought that this was a splendid answer.

Unfortunately, the critic was not mollified, and he said, "Well, you don't celebrate Good Friday like real Christians." Our wonderful new Latter-day Saint guide then said, "For us, the day Jesus died was Bad Friday, and we give our attention to the day He was resurrected: Good Sunday, or Easter." Another terrific answer. The man stayed a while longer but didn't ask this great group leader any more questions.

As we moved through the temple and were introduced to the baptistry and then the other sacred rooms and spaces, it seemed to me that there was a special spirit this good man brought to all of his clear and thoughtful responses to sincere questions that were asked. He concluded with a brief but touching testimony of Jesus Christ and the Restoration. I hope for all of us that each week is Holy Week and that we recognize what a privilege it is to celebrate "Good Sunday," or the Resurrection of the Lord.

As I have reflected on these experiences and others that I might relate, I have found new understanding in the words of the Prophet Joseph, who said: "The fundamental principles of our religion are the testimony of the Apostles and Prophets, concerning Jesus Christ, that He died, was buried, and rose again the third day, and ascended into heaven; and all other things which pertain to our religion are only appendages to it."[1]

Joseph Smith might have said that the fundamental principles of our religion are the *facts* or *evidence* concerning Jesus Christ, and I might not have initially appreciated any difference. But he did not choose those or other similar words. He said that the *testimonies* of the apostles and prophets concerning Jesus Christ provide the fundamental principles of our religion. I would likewise suggest that our own testimonies concerning Jesus Christ provide the basis of what is most dear to us.

Please do not misunderstand. Scholarship is essential and provides the framework to establish and protect our understanding of the unique mission and contributions of the Lord Jesus Christ. Without serious scholarship into the life and ministry of the Lord, our testimonies may be in peril or never established in the first instance. But scholarship alone does not provide the assurance that can come only from the true witness of the Holy Ghost. In fact, the nature of scholarship or research is that its conclusions are always tentative or incomplete, awaiting the next discovery, insight, or data. It is the testimony of Jesus, the spirit of prophecy (see Revelation 19:10), that brings full and unreserved confidence to our witness of Him.

We of all people welcome more knowledge and insight, but we also do not confuse even more robust understanding with the absolute conviction that can come only through the still, small voice whispered by the Holy Spirit. Thus, it is the testimony of apostles and prophets, as well as our personal testimonies, that cause us to be able to say without equivocation or reservation that Jesus is the Christ, our Savior and Redeemer, the Firstborn of the Father in the spirit world, and His Only Begotten Son in this mortal sphere.

That is why the fifteen living Apostles chose to share their testimonies in the wonderful document dated January 1, 2000, and entitled "The Living Christ: The Testimony of the Apostles, The Church of Jesus Christ of Latter-day Saints." They might have written books, indeed several have, that outlined the basis for their faith, understanding, and scholarship about Jesus. Interestingly, they decided to record their testimonies in thirteen brief paragraphs held to one page that also includes room for all fifteen signatures. Let me share again what they have written. I commend it to you as I bear my testimony of it and of Him:

Celebrating Easter

## THE LIVING CHRIST

As we commemorate the birth of Jesus Christ two millennia ago, we offer our testimony of the reality of His matchless life and the infinite virtue of His great atoning sacrifice. None other has had so profound an influence upon all who have lived and will yet live upon the earth.

He was the Great Jehovah of the Old Testament, the Messiah of the New. Under the direction of His Father, He was the creator of the earth. "All things were made by him; and without him was not any thing made that was made" (John 1:3). Though sinless, He was baptized to fulfill all righteousness. He "went about doing good" (Acts 10:38), yet was despised for it. His gospel was a message of peace and goodwill. He entreated all to follow His example. He walked the roads of Palestine, healing the sick, causing the blind to see, and raising the dead. He taught the truths of eternity, the reality of our premortal existence, the purpose of our life on earth, and the potential for the sons and daughters of God in the life to come.

He instituted the sacrament as a reminder of His great atoning sacrifice. He was arrested and condemned on spurious charges, convicted to satisfy a mob, and sentenced to die on Calvary's cross. He gave His life to atone for the sins of all mankind. His was a great vicarious gift in behalf of all who would ever live upon the earth.

We solemnly testify that His life, which is central to all human history, neither began in Bethlehem nor

## "Testimony of Jesus Christ"

concluded on Calvary. He was the Firstborn of the Father, the Only Begotten Son in the flesh, the Redeemer of the world.

He rose from the grave to "become the firstfruits of them that slept" (1 Corinthians 15:20). As Risen Lord, He visited among those He had loved in life. He also ministered among His "other sheep" (John 10:16) in ancient America. In the modern world, He and His Father appeared to the boy Joseph Smith, ushering in the long-promised "dispensation of the fulness of times" (Ephesians 1:10).

Of the Living Christ, the Prophet Joseph wrote: "His eyes were as a flame of fire; the hair of his head was white like the pure snow; his countenance shone above the brightness of the sun; and his voice was as the sound of the rushing of great waters, even the voice of Jehovah, saying:

"I am the first and the last; I am he who liveth, I am he who was slain; I am your advocate with the Father" (D&C 110:3–4).

Of Him the Prophet also declared: "And now, after the many testimonies which have been given of him, this is the testimony, last of all, which we give of him: That he lives!

"For we saw him, even on the right hand of God; and we heard the voice bearing record that he is the Only Begotten of the Father—

"That by him, and through him, and of him, the worlds are and were created, and the inhabitants thereof are begotten sons and daughters unto God" (D&C 76:22–24).

We declare in words of solemnity that His priesthood and His Church have been restored upon the earth—"built upon the foundation of . . . apostles and prophets, Jesus Christ himself being the chief corner stone" (Ephesians 2:20).

We testify that He will someday return to earth. "And the glory of the Lord shall be revealed, and all flesh shall see it together" (Isaiah 40:5). He will rule as King of Kings and reign as Lord of Lords, and every knee shall bend and every tongue shall speak in worship before Him. Each of us will stand to be judged of Him according to our works and the desires of our hearts.

We bear testimony, as His duly ordained Apostles—that Jesus is the Living Christ, the immortal Son of God. He is the great King Immanuel, who stands today on the right hand of His Father. He is the light, the life, and the hope of the world. His way is the path that leads to happiness in this life and eternal life in the world to come. God be thanked for the matchless gift of His divine Son.[2]

Now, this is the wonderful, moving, and affirmative testimony of the First Presidency and the Twelve. We understand that their testimonies are of special significance because these fifteen men are "special witnesses" (see D&C 107:23). For many in the world, including some who are striving for testimonies themselves, the witness of the Apostles is essential because these seeking people are the "others [to whom] it is given to believe on their words [meaning their testimony of Jesus Christ], that they also might have eternal life if they continue faithful" (D&C 46:14).

"Testimony of Jesus Christ"

I suppose some might think that because the scripture teaches that "To *some* it is given by the Holy Ghost to know that Jesus Christ is the Son of God, and that he was crucified for the sins of the world" (D&C 46:13; emphasis added), this must be an exclusive or restricted gift, perhaps even akin to the sectarian notion of predestination to salvation or damnation. Nothing could be further from the truth. While acquiring the testimony of Jesus may be easier for some than others, it is also abundantly clear that God wishes every person to have this witness and conviction personally.

Think of these remarkable words of counsel and promise given for our time in November 1831:

> Wherefore, I the Lord, knowing the calamity which should come upon the inhabitants of the earth, called upon my servant Joseph Smith, Jun., and spake unto him from heaven, and gave him commandments;
>
> And also gave commandments to others, that they should proclaim these things unto the world; and all this that it might be fulfilled, which was written by the prophets—
>
> The weak things of the world shall come forth and break down the mighty and strong ones, that man should not counsel his fellow man, neither trust in the arm of flesh—
>
> But that *every man* might speak in the name of God the Lord, even the Savior of the world;
>
> That faith also might increase in the earth. (D&C 1:17–21; emphasis added)

## Celebrating Easter

What a wonderful thing it would be if every man and woman could have the strength and conviction of their witness that they could confidently testify of truth in the name of the Savior! What a worthy goal for each of us and for each person that we have the occasion to touch and strengthen!

Each of us who has a testimony of Jesus as the Christ has a heavy and great responsibility to live our lives so that our conduct will match our convictions. As I bear again my witness of the literal, living reality of the resurrected Savior in our day, I also pray that we will do all that we can to build the testimonies of Jesus Christ in all with whom we are privileged to interact. Thanks to all of you who so magnificently and effectively testify of your knowledge and love of the Lord by the goodness of your example and precepts. This is His work, and He does watch over Israel. In the name of Jesus Christ, amen.

### NOTES

1. Joseph Smith, *History of the Church of Jesus Christ of Latter-day Saints*, ed. B. H. Roberts, 2nd ed. rev. (Salt Lake City: Deseret Book, 1980), 3:30.
2. The First Presidency and the Quorum of the Twelve, "The Living Christ: The Testimony of the Apostles, The Church of Jesus Christ of Latter-day Saints," *Ensign*, April 2000, 2.

JOHN S. TANNER

# Christ, Our Advocate and High Priest

Welcome to Easter Conference, the third in what I hope will be an enduring BYU tradition. This conference is held on the Saturday before Easter, a day that is typically treated by Latter-day Saints, who lack the tradition of Holy Week or Good Friday, as a weekend holiday for chores or recreation. This year the conference also happens to fall on April 15, tax day, the day when Americans respond to the edict of our empire that "all the world should be taxed" (Luke 2:1). I hope that this conference will help you meditate for a morning on the Mediator rather than on mammon, that it will provide a measure of spiritual re-creation to supplement your recreation, and that it will help transform a holiday weekend into

---

John S. Tanner is academic vice president at Brigham Young University.

a holy-day weekend. I thank in advance all those who will contribute to these ends.

The occasion of our holding an Easter conference on tax day reminds me of an Easter weekend almost four hundred years ago. On Good Friday in 1613, the poet John Donne found himself riding from London westward toward Wales on a business trip. Traditionally Good Friday is a day when the Christian world remembers the Crucifixion. It is a holy day in the Christian calendar, a solemn time when Christians are supposed to set aside worldly affairs, go to church, fast, pray, and reflect on the Savior's suffering and death. Instead, Donne devoted Good Friday, 1613, to his business obligations rather than to his religious duties. This circumstance became the occasion of one of the finest devotional poems in English, entitled "Good Friday, 1613. Riding Westward."[1]

In the poem, Donne laments, "I am carried towards the West / This day, when my soul's form bends toward the East." Then he engages in a complex but moving meditation on the Crucifixion. Donne travels in his mind from Wales back across the miles and the years to the foot of the cross. He can scarcely bear to look upon the agony there, as he imagines the Son of God "humbled below us." Donne sees in his mind "those hands, which [once] span[ned] the poles, / And tun[ed the] spheres," now "pierced with those holes"; "that blood," which is the source of eternal life, "made dirt of dust"; and "that flesh which was worn / By God for his apparel, ragg'd, and torn." Such a spectacle "made [Christ's] own lieutenant, Nature, shrink; / It made his footstool crack, and the sun wink." How then can Donne look upon Christ's face in agony? How can he watch his God die? Yet Donne forces himself to turn his imagined gaze up to Christ's face on the cross. As he does so, he imagines the Savior turning His gaze upon him, John Donne, a scandalously sinful man who, like Augustine, was notorious as a young man for having been often carried by "pleasure or business" westward into worldly ways when his soul should have inclined eastward toward the Savior. There follows this stunning conclusion, in which the poet pleads to be purified:

> Though these things, as I ride, be from mine eye,
> They are present yet unto my memory,
> For that looks towards them; and thou look'st towards me,
> O Savior, as thou hang'st upon the tree.
> I turn my back to thee but to receive
> Corrections, till thy mercies bid thee leave.
> O think me worth thine anger; punish me;
> Burn off my rusts and my deformity;
> Restore thine image so much, by thy grace,
> That thou may'st know me, and I'll turn my face.

Brothers and sisters, like Donne, all of us need the Savior to burn off the stains and rusts we accumulate in mortality. And we, too, must look to Christ to re-form by grace what we have de-formed by sin. May this hope for wholeness point our westward-wandering souls eastward toward a garden, a cross, and an empty tomb.

When we experience the purifying power of the Atonement, we may feel to exclaim with Enos, "Lord, how is it done?" (Enos 1:7). I know of no more compelling theological question in scripture than this. I want to give some perspective on this question today. Now, I do not claim to fully comprehend the awesome arithmetic of the Atonement by which one man's death adds up to life for all men, and a guiltless man's suffering cancels the guilt of all the penitent who come unto Him. Like Enos, I often wonder, "Lord, how is it done?"

Even so, I believe that scripture provides a remarkably intimate glimpse into the mechanics of mediation—that is, into how it is done—in its descriptions of Christ as our advocate and high priest. Scripture allows us to overhear the Son pleading our cause to the Father. It invites us to enter into the heavenly Holy of Holies, where God dwells with our great high priest and where every day is a Day of Atonement. The scriptures we will consider provide sacred glimpses into how it is done. So on this Saturday before Easter, let us mentally doff the shoes from off our feet and enter into the sanctuary where our salvation is wrought.

Traditionally, Christ is thought to have combined the three Old Testament offices of prophet, priest, and king. This triplet will be familiar to Latter-day Saints from the hymn "I Know That My Redeemer Lives," which appeared in the first Church hymnal: "He lives, my Prophet, Priest, and King."[2] As prophet, Christ is our teacher and exemplar whose words and actions reveal God's word to the world. As king, Christ is our ruler, judge, lawgiver, and Lord, into whose hands the Father has given the government of His kingdom. As priest, Christ is our redeemer, mediator, intercessor, and advocate with the Father, making a blood sacrifice that enables us to be cleansed from sin.

## "Christ, Our Advocate and High Priest"

Note that I subsume the role of advocate under the role of priest. I believe that this is consistent with scripture, particularly modern revelation. Modern revelation expands and greatly develops our understanding of Christ as advocate. Jesus is called advocate only once in the New Testament. This occurs in 1 John 2:1: "My little children, these things write I unto you, that ye sin not. And if any man sin, we have an advocate with the Father, Jesus Christ the righteous." Christ is alluded to as advocate many times in modern revelation. Modern revelation also clarifies even the verse in 1 John. The Joseph Smith Translation for this verse makes clear that Christ specifically acts as advocate for those who "sin *and repent.*"

*Advocate* denotes not merely a lawyer but literally one who speaks for us. The word comes from the Latin *ad vocare,* "to speak for." First John 2:1 employs the Greek term *parakletos,* which connotes one who is at our side, sometimes translated as "our helper." The same Greek term is used for the Holy Ghost in His role as comforter. The idea here is that Christ is by our side, as our helper and our defender; He speaks in our behalf.

The fullest and most intimate description of Christ as advocate in modern revelation occurs in Doctrine and Covenants 45:3–5. I have come to regard this passage much as I do Doctrine and Covenants 19:15–20, in which the Savior recounts His atoning sacrifice, "Which suffering caused myself, even God, . . . to tremble because of pain." Both passages are remarkably intimate, first-person descriptions by the Savior of the Atonement. In Doctrine and Covenants 45, the Savior describes His sacred, saving interaction with the Father: "Listen to him who is the advocate with the Father, who is pleading your cause before him—saying: Father, behold the sufferings and death of him who did no sin, in whom thou wast well pleased; behold the blood of thy Son which was shed, the blood of him whom thou gavest that thyself might be glorified; wherefore, Father, spare these my brethren that believe on my name, that they may come unto me and have everlasting life" (vv. 3–5). So many things are noteworthy about this passage. Let me mention several.

1. Note the present tense: Christ *is* pleading our cause—this is His constant, ongoing activity before the Father. Likewise, He points to His suffering, death, and blood as if they were present for the Father's contemplation: "behold the sufferings," "behold the . . . death." As in Donne's poem, it is as if the Son and the Father are reliving the great agony in the garden and on the cross in an eternal present. In his discussion of this idea, Elder Neal A. Maxwell notes the "ongoingness" of Christ's atoning advocacy for us.[3]

2. Note the emphasis: it falls almost entirely on the Savior's redemptive suffering and only minimally on our actions. He asks the Father to spare us based on His merits, not on ours. We have a part to play in this divine drama of salvation, to be sure. Our role is briefly acknowledged in the phrase those "that believe on my name." But what we must do—believe—seems so small, insignificant, and disproportionate compared to what must be done for us that it is almost embarrassing. We, as believers, are the beneficiaries of the Son's suffering and death, His perfect life, and His shed blood—not to mention the Father's sacrifice in giving such a Son to be so treated for the sake of our salvation.

## "Christ, Our Advocate and High Priest"

3. Note the word *wherefore*: surely there is not a more crucial *wherefore* in all scripture than that in verse 5. It links the Son's suffering to an appeal to the Father to spare us. This simple causal conjunction denotes the reason the Father should consider this appeal. The hopes of every believer hinge upon this *wherefore*.

4. Note that Jesus calls us familiarly "my brethren": of course, Latter-day Saints know that this is literally true—we are all spiritual sons and daughters of God. Christ is the firstborn and therefore our eldest brother. Nevertheless, in context, this does not sound like a mere statement of fact. Rather, it sounds here as if Christ were reminding the Father of His kinship with us, as if we were coequal siblings rather than utterly dependent petitioners. Jesus does not have to designate us "my brethren." He could just as well name us "these poor sinners" or even "these thy children." Instead, He expresses solidarity with fallen humanity—with us!—in the words "these my brethren." What a condescending, merciful, gracious phrase! Here is an advocate who loves us even though He knows full well our weaknesses, for He has taken upon Himself our infirmities. Here is an advocate who knows how to succor us. As the Lord says in Doctrine and Covenants 62:1, "Behold, and hearken, O ye elders of my church, saith the Lord your God, even Jesus Christ, your advocate, who knoweth the weakness of man and how to succor them who are tempted."

5. Note that He pleads for grace for those "that believe on my name" (present tense) in order "that they may come unto me" (future tense): the first relative clause describes the present condition of the redeemed—they are believers. The second anticipates their future conditions—as those

who have been forgiven and are thus enabled to come unto Him and inherit eternal life. As our advocate, Christ pleads not only for our forgiveness or justification but ultimately for our sanctification. His intercession thus both spares us from punishment *and* enables us to come unto Him and have eternal life. It opens the door for at-one-ment with Father and Son.

6. Finally, note that both here and elsewhere in scripture Christ is always portrayed as our advocate *with the Father*: in some ways the relationship between the Son and Father is the most surprising and potentially puzzling feature of the doctrine of Christ as advocate. What is the role of the Father in relation to Christ as advocate? Is the Father to be considered our accuser, who stands in opposition to our advocate? No, this role belongs to Satan (see Revelation 12:10). The very word *devil* (*diabolos*) means "accuser or slanderer." If the Father is not our accuser, is He then a stern, just judge who must be placated by a Son who advocates for mercy? Yes and no. The scriptures sometimes suggest this, as in Doctrine and Covenants 109 when Joseph prays that the Father "wilt turn away thy wrath when thou lookest upon the face of thine Anointed" (v. 53). Scripture contains several similar passages that could lead one to attribute mercy and justice to separate members of the Godhead. But surely it would be a mistake to imagine that the Father embodies merely justice and vengeance while the Son embodies exclusively mercy and compassion. Just as the Son is both our merciful advocate and our just judge, so the Father possesses in Himself the qualities of both justice and mercy in perfect fullness. One member of the Godhead is not more merciful or just than

the other. To the extent that Christ acts as our advocate for mercy with His Father, He summons forth mercy that already exists in His Father's heart.

But I think there is yet another way of looking at this divine drama between the advocate Son and His Father. I believe that as our advocate *with the Father*, Christ is not so much placating a wrathful God as He is claiming His rights under the covenant—the new covenant—to redeem those who repent. This covenant and these rights are predicated on the blood of one who "did no sin." Through the Atonement, Jesus earned a place at "the right hand of God," as Mormon says, "to claim of the Father his rights of mercy . . . ; wherefore he advocateth the cause of the children of men" (Moroni 7:27–28). Likewise, as Jesus tells the Prophet Joseph Smith, "I am Christ, and . . . by the virtue of the blood which I have spilt, have I pleaded before the Father for them" (D&C 38:4). As advocate, Jesus claims His rights of mercy with the Father, which He earned by virtue of the blood He spilt for us.

This is the way I read the extraordinary first-person glimpse we get from Doctrine and Covenants 45 into the Savior's role as our advocate *with the Father*. In effect, Christ is saying to His Father, "Behold the fearful price that has been paid for salvation; wherefore spare these my beloved brothers and sisters who believe in me so that they may become one with us and receive eternal life."

As advocate, Christ intercedes for us as our great high priest. He prays to the Father "for them . . . which shall believe on me" (John 17:20): "Sanctify them through thy truth: . . . that they may be one; as thou, Father, art in me, and I in thee, that they may also be one in us . . . that they may be made perfect in one" (John 17:17, 21, 23). Advocate and priest are both intercessory and mediatorial priestly offices.

Let me now speak briefly about the Savior's role as *high priest*. This is described most fully, of course, in the Epistle to the Hebrews. In fact, it forms the controlling idea of Paul's epistle. Paul recognized that the high priest who entered into the Holy of Holies on the Day of Atonement was but a "shadow of heavenly things" (Hebrews 8:5). In New Testament times, once a year, the high priest entered the Holy of Holies in the temple with a censer of incense to make a blood offering that would cleanse the people from sin. Paul explains that, similarly, as high priest Christ has entered the Holy of Holies in heaven through the offering of His own blood. He combines in Himself, as it were, the role of both priest and sacrificial animal: "Neither by the blood of goats and calves, but by his own blood he entered in once into the holy place, having obtained eternal redemption for us" (Hebrews 9:12). "For Christ is not entered into the holy places made with hands, which are figures of the true; but into heaven itself, now to appear in the presence of God for us" (Hebrews 9:24).

But this is not all. Not only has Christ entered a heavenly Holy of Holies for us, He has made it possible for us to enter too. In ancient Israel only the high priest could pass through the second veil into this inner sanctuary where stood the mercy seat. Christ's atoning sacrifice has opened the sanctuary of God to all believers. Paul says that Christ opened unto us "a new and living way" (Hebrews 10:20), through the veil of His own flesh and own blood, whereby we can enter the holiest place. "Therefore, brethren," Paul goes on to say, let us have "boldness to enter into the holiest by the blood of Jesus" (Hebrews 10:19).

This understanding of Christ as our great high priest and advocate offers stunning, sweet, and hopeful doctrine. It has caused me to pray more earnestly of late for forgiveness through the atoning blood of Christ. I have echoed in my devotions the prayers of the people of Benjamin: "O have mercy, and apply the atoning blood of Christ that we may receive forgiveness of our sins, and our hearts may be purified; for we believe in Jesus Christ, the Son of God" (Mosiah 4:2).

I have imagined the Savior, as advocate and high priest, coming before the Father to plead for me. How grateful I have felt to have such an advocate, "who knoweth the weakness of man and how to succor them who are tempted" (D&C 62:1). Likewise, I take comfort in Paul's descriptions of Christ as high priest, who "took not on him the nature of angels" but was "made like unto his brethren, that he might be a merciful . . . high priest. . . . For in that he himself hath suffered being tempted, he is able to succour them that are tempted" (Hebrews 2:16–18). Consequently, he "can have compassion on . . . them that are out of the way; for he himself also is compassed with infirmity" (Hebrews 5:2). This knowledge ought to embolden us to come to the Father's throne: "For we have not an high priest which cannot be touched with the feeling of our infirmities; but was in all points tempted like as we are, yet without sin. Let us therefore come boldly unto the throne of grace, that we may obtain mercy, and find grace to help in time of need" (Hebrews 4:15–16).

Celebrating Easter

I began with quoting a great seventeenth-century religious poet. Let me end with another: John Milton. At the end of *Paradise Lost,* Milton beautifully describes the Son acting in the priestly office as intercessor and advocate in behalf of fallen Adam and Eve, who have just offered a heartfelt, penitent prayer consisting not only of words but of unutterable sighs. These ascend to heaven, where Christ, "their great Intercessor," clad like a priest with incense, comes before the Father's throne and says:

> See Father, what first-fruits on earth are sprung
> From thy implanted grace in man, these sighs
> And prayers, which in this golden censer, mixed
> With incense, I thy priest before thee bring,
> Fruits of more pleasing savor from thy seed
> Sown with contrition in his heart, than those
> Which his own hand manuring all the trees
> Of Paradise could have produced, ere fall'n
> From innocence. Now therefore bend thine ear
> To supplication, hear his sighs though mute;
> Unskilful with what words to pray, let me
> Interpret for him, me his advocate
> And propitiation...
> Let him live
>
> Before thee reconciled....
> To better life shall yield him, where with me
> All my redeemed may dwell in joy and bliss,
> Made one with me as I with thee am one.
>
> To whom the Father [answers]...
> All thy request for Man, accepted Son,
> Obtain, all thy request was my decree.[4]

## "Christ, Our Advocate and High Priest"

I testify that Christ is our advocate and priest. He pleads for us. He prays for us with the Father. He has entered the heavenly Holy of Holies through His own blood and made Atonement so that we can have "the boldness to enter into the holiest by the blood of Jesus." "Oh, it is wonderful, wonderful to me!"[5]

### NOTES

1. All quotes from the poem are in *The Norton Anthology of English Literature*, 5th ed. (New York: Norton, 1986), 1:101–2.
2. Samuel Medley, "I Know That My Redeemer Lives," *Hymns* (Salt Lake City: The Church of Jesus Christ of Latter-day Saints, 1985), no. 136.
3. Neal A. Maxwell, *One More Strain of Praise* (Salt Lake City: Deseret Book, 1999), 44–45.
4. Milton, *Paradise Lost*, book 11, lines 22–47 (see Thomas H. Luxon, ed., *The Milton Reading Room*, www.dartmouth.edu/~milton, accessed January 2007).
5. Charles H. Gabriel, "I Stand All Amazed," *Hymns*, no. 193.

TERRY B. BALL

# The Unique and Supreme Attributes of Jesus the Christ

During Alma's ministry among the people of Ammonihah, he taught them of the priesthood to which he was ordained, which both authorized and mandated him to teach God's commandments. He testified that the "Lord God ordained priests, after his holy order, which was after the order of his Son, to teach" the commandments of God to the people (Alma 13:1). He then explained, "And this is the manner after which they were ordained—being called and prepared from the foundation of the world according to the foreknowledge of God, on account of their exceeding faith and good works; in the first place being left to choose good or evil; therefore they having chosen good, and exercising exceedingly great faith, are called with a holy calling" (v. 3).

---

Terry B. Ball is dean of Religious Education at Brigham Young University.

Alma's understanding that those ordained to the high priesthood were so ordained on account of their "exceeding faith ... in the first place," raises some provocative questions. For example, "in the first place," which we understand to be the premortal life, God "stood in the midst" of the "noble and great ones" that were "chosen" before they were born (Abraham 3:22–23). Elder Bruce R. McConkie explained that "in the premortal life *we all* dwelt in his [God's] presence, saw his face, and heard his voice."[1] Under such circumstances, in what, then, did those foreordained to the high priesthood exercise faith that qualified them for this distinction? If we understand, as Alma taught, that "faith is not to have a perfect knowledge of things" but rather a "hope for things which are not seen" (Alma 32:21), then the faith exercised by those foreordained to the high priesthood in the premortal life must have been something other than faith in the existence of God, for there they dwelt with God and saw Him. They would have had a perfect knowledge of His existence. What was it then that they hoped for but had not yet seen?

Certainly one unseen truth in which they must have exercised faith was that Jesus, He who was "chosen from the beginning" by the Father (Moses 4:2), really could and would be able to work the great, infinite Atonement that was such a vital part of God's plan. They must have believed that He truly could and would do the will of the Father, that He truly could and would be our Savior, and that He truly could and would live a sinless life and suffer and die for us.

This conclusion leads to another important question: why? Why in that premortal setting did they—and for that matter, why did all of us before we were born to this earth—have faith in Jesus, faith that He could and would be our Redeemer? I believe one answer is that we recognized then, as we recognize now in mortality, attributes in Jesus that identify Him as one both uniquely and supremely prepared and qualified to be our Savior. We must have believed what Cecil F. Alexander declared in her hymn, "There was no other good enough to pay the price of sin. He only could unlock the gate of heav'n and let us in."[2]

## JESUS'S PREMORTAL AND MORTAL ATTRIBUTES

*The Firstborn and Only Begotten.* As Latter-day Saints, we hold as true Jesus's pronouncement "I was in the beginning with the Father, and am the Firstborn" (D&C 93:21; compare Romans 8:29; Colossians 1:15), meaning the Firstborn of all God the Father's premortal spirit children.[3] We further understand that because He was chosen to be our Savior, in mortality He also became the "only begotten" in the flesh (see John 1:14, 18; John 3:16; 1 John 4:9).[4] Furthermore, we know that when He was born in mortality Jesus fulfilled the prophecy of Micah (see Micah 5:2), for He was born in Bethlehem, the city of David (see Luke 2:4–6). Thus, Jesus is both unique and supreme among God's children being the Firstborn in the spirit and the Only Begotten in the flesh, born in Bethlehem in fulfillment of prophecy.

*The glory and image of the Father.* The first chapter of Hebrews informs us that Jesus was "the brightness of his [God the Father's] glory, and the express image of his person" (Hebrews 1:2–3; compare John 1:14). Speaking of Their appearance, Joseph Smith taught that the Father and the Son "exactly resembled each other in features and likeness."[5] Perhaps this is why, in mortality, Jesus could declare to Philip, "He that hath seen me hath seen the Father" (John 14:9). While He may have maintained His physical resemblance to the Father as He ministered in the flesh, Christ apparently did not openly go about displaying the "brightness" of the Father's glory to which He had attained in His premortal life, for Isaiah prophesied that in mortality "he hath no form nor comeliness; and when we shall see him, there is no beauty that we should desire him" (Isaiah 53:2).[6] Speaking of the remarkable contrast between the premortal and mortal Jesus's status and glory, Elder Francis M. Gibbons testified, "The supernal status of our Savior, Jesus Christ, and the preeminent place which he occupies in the eternal scheme of things cause us to stand in awe at what has been called the condescension of Christ, meaning his willingness to step down from his exalted place and to go forth, as the scripture says, 'suffering pains and afflictions and temptations of every kind; . . . that he may loose the bands of death which bind his people; and he will take upon him their infirmities, that his bowels may be filled with mercy, according to the flesh, that he may know according to the flesh how to succor his people according to their infirmities, . . . that he might blot out their transgressions according to the power of his deliverance' (Alma 7:11–13)."[7] Once again, Jesus presents both a unique and supreme attribute in that not only does He resemble the Father in appearance but also in brightness and glory—a glory which He set aside to minister in the flesh. No other child of God has condescended more, for no one could have given up more to become mortal.

*In the beginning with God.* The Gospel of John adds considerably to our understanding of Jesus's premortal attributes, accomplishments, and stature. As John opens his Gospel, he declares that Jesus, whom he calls the "Word," was "in the beginning" (John 1:1; compare D&C 93:6–8). We understand this to mean that He was not a latecomer to God's work and plans. He was not, as some early Christian sects would try to explain, simply a man who lived such a good life in mortality that God chose to put His Spirit in Him.[8] Rather, Jesus was as Moses explains "chosen from the beginning" (Moses 4:2). John further testifies that not only was Jesus present from the beginning but also that He was "with God" (John 1:1). I believe this is more a statement of commitment than of simple presence. In other words, He was not just simply present with the Father but He was "with" Him in thought, purpose, and will—so much so that in mortality He could testify, "I and my Father are one" (John 10:30). No other person born to this earth has so totally conformed to the Father's will that he or she could so rightfully make such a claim in mortality.

*The Great Jehovah.* John further declares that not only was Jesus with God in the beginning but that "the Word was God" (John 1:1; compare D&C 38:1–5). Latter-day Saints understand this to mean that somehow even before He came to earth Jesus had attained unto the stature of a God—divinely invested by God the Father with the authority to be Jehovah, the God of the Old Testament. As Jesus Himself testified in a revelation to the Prophet Joseph Smith, "Thus saith the Lord your God, even Jesus

Christ, the Great *I Am*, Alpha and Omega, the beginning and the end, the same which looked upon the wide expanse of eternity, and all the seraphic hosts of heaven, before the world was made; the same which knoweth all things, for all things are present before mine eyes; I am the same which spake, and the world was made, and all things came by me. I am the same which have taken the Zion of Enoch into mine own bosom; and verily, I say, even as many as have believed in my name, for I am Christ" (D&C 38:1–4). Jesus wants us to understand that He is the God who spoke to Abraham, Isaac, and Jacob; the God who parted the Red Sea and brought down the walls of Jericho; and the God who became flesh and dwelt among us (see John 1:14). Thus, He could testify through Isaiah, "I, even I, am [Jehovah]; and beside me there is no saviour" (Isaiah 43:11).[9]

*The Creator.* John continues his description of Jesus's attributes by explaining that He also had a role in the Creation. John testified, "All things were made by him; and without him was not any thing made that was made" (John 1:3). Moses further clarifies Jesus's role in the Creation, teaching us that Jesus created the worlds under the direction of the Father: "And by the word of my power, have I created them, which is mine Only Begotten Son, who is full of grace and truth. And worlds without number have I created; and I also created them for mine own purpose; and by the Son I created them, which is mine Only Begotten" (Moses 1:32–33). How appropriate that He who was in the beginning; who was with God in every way; who was Jehovah, the God of the Old Testament; and who was the creator of the earth, should also be chosen to be its Savior.

# "Unique & Supreme Attributes of Jesus the Christ"

## The Life and Light of Men

Continuing to describe Jesus's attributes and "credentials," John says of Him, "In him was life; and the life was the light of men" (John 1:4). By life, I believe John means something far more than mortal life; rather, that Jesus is the means whereby we have access to eternal life. By light, I believe John means light as defined in Doctrine and Covenants 93: Jesus is the source of truth, knowledge, and intelligence (see D&C 93:24–37). John further explained that the "true Light" of Jesus "lighteth every man that cometh into the world" (John 1:9). What a remarkable and essential attribute for the Savior to have—the ability to give light, truth, intelligence, and ultimately eternal life to all of us.[10] John then describes the blessings that can be ours if we accept the light and truth Jesus offers. John promises, "But as many as received him, to them gave he power to become the sons of God, even to them that believe on his name" (John 1:12). This promise tells us that if we are willing to accept Jesus and the light and life He offers, then we become like Him—children of God just as Jesus is and heirs to all that the Father has. As the revelation on the priesthood assures us, "He that receiveth me receiveth my Father; and he that receiveth my Father receiveth my Father's kingdom; therefore all that my Father hath shall be given unto him" (D&C 84:37–38). It is my faith that only Jesus could offer this to us. It is only through believing on and receiving Jesus, His gospel, and His Atonement that we can become heirs to all the Father has. As Nephi declared, "And now, behold, my beloved brethren, this is the way; and there is none other way nor name given under heaven whereby man can be saved in the kingdom of God" (2 Nephi 31:21).

## CONCLUSION

While this discussion of Jesus's attributes is intended to be illustrative rather than exhaustive, I hope it is adequate to support the truth that Jesus, He who was known in mortality as Jesus of Nazareth, was both uniquely and supremely qualified to be our Savior. He truly was the Firstborn and Only Begotten of the Father. He was with the Father from the beginning. He was even like the Father—one with Him in love, purpose, power, and will—so much so that He was divinely invested with the authority to be Jehovah, the God of the Old Testament, who created the world and offered it light, truth, intelligence, and eternal life. He condescended to come to earth as a mortal man of ordinary appearance and to become like His brethren in all things (see Hebrews 2:17). As Alma declared, He suffered pains, afflictions, and temptations of every kind, and ultimately death so He could loose the bands of death (see Alma 7:11–12). I believe in the premortal council when He was chosen to be our Savior each of us born to this earth agreed with the choice. We had faith in Him. We believed that He was good, that He was wise, and that He loved us. As Cecil Alexander declared and as we recognized in that heavenly council, "There was no other good enough to pay the price of sin. He only could unlock the gate of heav'n and let us in."

## NOTES

1. Bruce R. McConkie, *A New Witness for the Articles of Faith* (Salt Lake City: Deseret Book, 1985), 45; emphasis added. See also Sterling W. Sill, in *Conference Report*, October 1956, 66.

2. "There Is a Green Hill Far Away," *Hymns* (Salt Lake City: The Church of Jesus Christ of Latter-day Saints, 1985), no. 194.

3. While Romans 8:29 identifies Jesus as the firstborn "among many brethren," and Colossians 1:15 is understood by some to also mean the firstborn from the grave in the resurrection, Elder Joseph B. Wirthlin helps us understand that Jesus was indeed "the Firstborn Son of our Heavenly Father in the spirit" ("Christians in Belief and Action," *Ensign*, November 1996, 70).

4. See also Topical Guide, "Jesus Christ, Only Begotten Son," 251.

5. Joseph Smith, *History of the Church of Jesus Christ of Latter-day Saints*, ed. B. H. Roberts, 2nd ed. rev. (Salt Lake City: Deseret Book, 1957), 4:536.

6. Isaiah uses the past tense or "prophetic perfect" in this prophecy, "speaking of things to come as though they had already come" (Mosiah 16:6). For other descriptions of Jesus's glorified premortal and postmortal appearance see the Topical Guide under the headings "Jesus Christ, Appearances, Antemortal" and "Jesus Christ, Appearance, Postmortal."

7. Francis M. Gibbons, "The Savior and Joseph Smith—Alike yet Unlike," *Ensign*, May 1991, 33.

8. This was a belief held by some Gnostic Christians. For a discussion of the issue, see Bart D. Ehrman, *The New Testament: A Historical Introduction to the Early Christian Writings*, 3rd ed. (New York: Oxford University Press, 2004), 6–7, 191.
9. Here I have chosen to interpret the tetragrammaton, the name of the God of the Old Testament, as Jehovah, rather than following the KJV practice of translating the term as "the Lord."
10. For more discussion on this topic see Dallin H. Oaks, "The Light and Life of the World," *Ensign*, November 1987, 63.

RUSSELL C. RASMUSSEN

# THE DILEMMA: AN INCOMPREHENSIBLE ATONEMENT?

Early in my life I experienced a dilemma regarding the Atonement that made it difficult for me to understand and utilize its power. I often heard Church leaders and seminary teachers talk about the "incomprehensible" nature of the Atonement. They would describe the Atonement as so grand and great and godlike that it is impossible for mortals to understand it fully. They would in the next breath state that the Atonement was the central doctrine of the Church and that we must know and understand it in order to experience forgiveness, peace, and direction in this life and exaltation in the life after.

This dilemma caused me at once to feel a deep reverence for the Atonement and to convince myself

---

Russell C. Rasmussen is manager of visitors' centers, historic sites, and pageants for the LDS Church and is a part-time instructor of ancient scripture at Brigham Young University.

that in order to understand it and experience its full blessings I would need either to become a prophet or wait until I died. This contradiction prevented the Atonement from affecting my life.

I have since spoken to many others who have struggled with similar thoughts and emotions. People often talk about the Atonement in lofty terms, but when it comes to the personal effects of the Atonement—regularly experiencing the peace and joy from cleansing and healing—these same people feel that they are not spiritually prepared and that they can only complete this preparation sometime in the future, when they are wiser and more perfect.

How can we speak about both the incomprehensible and the comprehensible nature of the Atonement at the same time—in the same phrase—and consider both descriptions at once right and good? For me the answer to this dilemma came from the scriptures and through the living prophets of God. These essential sources helped me begin to understand the purpose and significance of the Atonement as an essential doctrine of the gospel and, more specifically, as a doctrine that could help me personally right now.

## THE ATONEMENT AS CENTRAL AND ESSENTIAL DOCTRINE

To clarify, when the word *Atonement* is used in this article it refers to the experience of Jesus Christ in the Garden of Gethsemane and on the cross of Calvary, where in both places He suffered for the sin, sickness, and inadequacy of His people (see Alma 7:11; Matthew 26:35–45; Mark 14:32).

## "The Dilemma: An Incomprehensible Atonement?"

The Church of Jesus Christ of Latter-day Saints views the Atonement of Jesus Christ as the central and single most important doctrine in the gospel. This is affirmed in everything from the Prophet Joseph Smith's testimony of "Jesus Christ, that he died, was buried, and rose again the third day . . . and all other things which pertain to our religion are only appendages,"[1] to the title page of the Book of Mormon, which states that one of its major purposes is "convincing . . . that Jesus is the Christ" (see also 2 Nephi 26:12).

Since the earth's beginning, starting with Adam, prophets have taught and testified of Jesus Christ. As Jacob said, "Behold, I say unto you that *none* of the prophets have written, nor prophesied, *save they have spoken concerning this Christ*" (Jacob 7:11; emphasis added). Not just a few prophets have testified of Christ: all of the prophets on this earth have spoken or written about Christ. Helaman stated that "there is no other way nor means whereby man can be saved, only through the atoning blood of Jesus Christ" (Helaman 5:9). Nephi taught, "We talk of Christ, we rejoice in Christ, we preach of Christ, we prophesy of Christ" (2 Nephi 25:26). Alma points out what many prophets have said regarding the singularity of Jesus Christ: "There be many things to come; and behold, there is one thing which is of more importance than they all . . . that the Redeemer liveth and cometh among his people" (Alma 7:7). These verses, with a multitude of others in scripture, establish for us a foundation: the Atonement of Jesus Christ truly is the central and most essential doctrine of this gospel.

The testimonies of the prophets, the centrality of the Atonement in the gospel and in the Book of Mormon, and searching the scriptures took me from thinking that I simply needed to be familiar with the story of Jesus Christ to finally understanding that what Christ had accomplished through the Atonement was essential for my salvation. "For it is expedient that an atonement should be made; for according to the great plan of the Eternal God there must be an atonement made, or else all mankind must unavoidably perish" (Alma 34:9). Words such as "expedient," "must," "all mankind," and "unavoidably" testify that the Atonement is not meant for mere religion hobbyists but is absolutely necessary for us all.

## THE INCOMPREHENSIBLE NATURE OF THE ATONEMENT

Having now identified the Atonement as central and essential, the question follows: is the Atonement incomprehensible? The easy answer is yes—parts of it are incomprehensible. There are aspects of the Atonement that are not possible for us to understand fully right now; but it is not because we as mortals lack the necessary intelligence. It is not because God does not trust us with that knowledge or because we are not spiritual enough. As natural, mortal men and women, we do not have the capacity to comprehend the totality of the Atonement. That knowledge will come at some point after this life, when "knowing all things," as our Heavenly Father does, becomes possible for us (Moroni 7:22). Until we reach such a point, we must do as King Benjamin instructed and "believe in God; believe that he is, and that he created all things," but also "believe that man doth not comprehend

## "The Dilemma: An Incomprehensible Atonement?"

all the things which the Lord can comprehend" (Mosiah 4:9). In that light, let us examine those aspects of the Atonement that are often considered incomprehensible.

*Infinite.* "Therefore there can be nothing which is short of an infinite atonement which will suffice for the sins of the world" (Alma 34:12). We can, of course, understand the mathematical definition of the word "infinite," but as mortals we cannot quite wrap our minds around the literal truth of a thing that continues forever. Nearly everything that surrounds us in this life has an end. There is an end to childhood; there is an end to every career; there is an end to physical prowess, agility, and strength; and, of course, there is an end to our mortal lives. *Finite* is a concept we understand completely.

It takes an "infinite atonement" and nothing less to overcome the sins of the entire world. Think of the tragedy of a *finite* atonement. A finite atonement would have a limit to its ability to encompass all sin. What if, for example, the Atonement had a maximum quantitative capacity, beyond which its power could not reach. If that maximum capacity were, say, six billion sins, it would be sad for the individual whose sin reached 6,000,000,001. The Atonement cannot be finite because God's power and ability are limitless, infinite.[2]

I was never good at math in school, but there was one concept I did understand. Adding any number—great or small—to infinity always equals infinity. Expand that concept, and simple math such as the addition, subtraction, multiplication, or division of any number by infinity will always yield infinity.[3] Now, reconsider the individual whose sin was number 6,000,000,001. Place all 6,000,000,001 sins next to an infinite atonement, and they are completely "swallowed up" (Mosiah 15:7) by the Atonement's very infinite nature.

Consider also the capacity of an infinite atonement as it relates to time. The scriptures tell us that time constrains only those of us here on this earth (see Alma 40:8), and therefore we speak about things as being in the past, present, or future. With a finite atonement, time would place a constraint on the capacity of the Atonement because it would demand that only those sins occurring after the actual act of the Atonement could rightfully claim the power of the Atonement. Sins committed before the actual act of the Atonement would not be eligible to receive its power. So another facet of an infinite atonement is the fact that time is not relevant. All those who have lived, are living, or will live can access the power of the Atonement for redemption from sin (see Mosiah 3:13; Jarom 1:11; Alma 39:15–19).

*Forgiveness and resurrection.* As mortals, we are prey to both physical and spiritual death. Both deaths become like a cavernous pit with walls so high that we cannot climb out. We are trapped with no hope of escape unless someone outside the pit has ropes or ladders to get us out. "O how great the goodness of our God, who prepareth a way for our escape from the grasp of this awful monster . . . which I call the death of the body, and also the death of the spirit" (2 Nephi 9:10). The source of our escape comes through Jesus Christ, the Son of God, the Savior who would "atone for the sins of the world" (Alma 34:8) and who "bringeth to pass the resurrection of the dead" (Mosiah 15:20).

## "The Dilemma: An Incomprehensible Atonement?"

But with the relief that comes from the possibility of rescue also comes another dilemma: how can the suffering and death of one individual allow another individual to overcome sin and death? Amulek explored this same question: "Now there is not any man that can sacrifice his own blood which will atone for the sins of another" (Alma 34:11). There is simply no human being who can sacrifice his or her own blood to atone for the sins of someone else. As Amulek taught, if a man murders, the life of someone else cannot pay for the murder; only the life of the man who committed the murder can atone for his crime, though even that falls short (see Alma 34:11–12).[4] There really is only one way: "Therefore there can be nothing which is short of an infinite atonement which will suffice for the sins of the world" (Alma 34:12), "for it shall not be a human sacrifice; but it must be an infinite and eternal sacrifice" (v. 10).

Elder James E. Talmage addresses the incomprehensible nature of the covering of our sins through the Atonement: "In some manner, actual and terribly real though to man incomprehensible, the Savior took upon Himself the burden of the sins of mankind from Adam to the end of the world."[5] And Elder Bruce R. McConkie emphasizes that "in some way incomprehensible to us, the effects of [Christ's] resurrection pass upon all men so that all shall rise from the grave."[6] We simply will not understand these things completely until we become like our Heavenly Father.

*Performed by a God.* While the scriptures tell us of God, our Heavenly Father, and His Son, Jesus Christ (see Moroni 7:2, 48), and describe some of their characteristics and attributes (see D&C 29:1; Alma 32:22; 2 Nephi 9:20; Ether 3:12), we cannot fully understand all that it means to be God: "Behold, great and marvelous are the works of the Lord. How unsearchable are the depths of the mysteries of him; and it is impossible that man should find out all his ways" (Jacob 4:8). Moses learned this truth from experience when God told him, "I will show thee the workmanship of mine hands; but not all, for my works are without end, and also my words. . . . The heavens, they are many, and they cannot be numbered unto man" (Moses 1:4, 37).

Although He lived on the earth as a mortal, we see in Jesus the capacity of a God. That ability was made possible because of the nature of His Father, God the Father (see Alma 7:10; Mosiah 3:8; 15:3; D&C 93:4). Jesus's divine attributes and capacity were absolutely essential for Him to survive the physically, emotionally, and spiritually taxing Atonement in all its infinite complexities. "And lo, he shall suffer temptations, and pain of body, hunger, thirst, and fatigue, even more than man can suffer, except it be unto death" (Mosiah 3:7). During the experience of the Atonement, the Savior went through extreme pain and suffering, "which suffering caused [Himself], even God, the greatest of all, to tremble because of pain" (D&C 19:18). King Benjamin teaches that we could not experience this type of pain because a mere mortal would die before ever reaching the necessary point of extremity (see Mosiah 3:7). In the words of Elder Henry B. Eyring, "He worked out the Atonement . . . [that] was so painful and so terrible that we cannot comprehend it."[7]

Any attempts made by us to duplicate and therefore understand by experience what Christ went through is

## "The Dilemma: An Incomprehensible Atonement?"

simply not possible because we are mortals, not Gods. All of our possible strengths combined would fall far short of what the Atonement required. Again, Amulek explains "it must be an infinite and eternal sacrifice," which "sacrifice will be the Son of God" (Alma 34:10, 14) to satisfy the Atonement's requirements.

### THE COMPREHENSIBLE NATURE OF THE ATONEMENT

We have addressed several aspects of the Atonement that are incomprehensible to us. But is there anything about the Atonement that is comprehensible? The qualified answer is yes—parts of it.

One might wonder if it is even worthwhile to try to comprehend the Atonement because, after all, we are imperfect and mortal beings. But that is precisely the point. Because we are imperfect and mortal, we desperately need to comprehend how the Atonement affects us now. We find in the scriptures the commandment given by God to "come unto Christ ... and partake of his salvation, and the power of his redemption" (Omni 1:26), and to "be reconciled unto him [Heavenly Father] through the atonement of Christ, his Only Begotten Son" (Jacob 4:11). A degree of comprehension, then, must be both possible and attainable, for we are told that the Lord will not give commandments to us unless it is possible to keep those commandments (see 1 Nephi 3:7; 17:50).

God tells us further that when He asks us to do something and promises blessings dependent on our obedience, then "he will fulfil all his promises which he shall make unto you" (Alma 37:17) because "he never doth vary from that which he hath said" (Mosiah 2:22). So when He says to come unto Him and be reconciled through His Atonement, we must trust that there is a way for us to do just that and that God will help us fulfill that command.

We are told further that obtaining eternal life depends on us knowing Heavenly Father and Jesus Christ (see John 17:3; D&C 132:24). Knowing is a combination of learning about Christ and His ways and learning to do what He would do (see D&C 130:18–19). In our quest to comprehend the Atonement and to enjoy its blessings now, Heavenly Father has given us principles, doctrines, ordinances, and other tools to help us.

## THE DOCTRINE OF CHRIST

Stepping-stones are laid out before us to help us understand the Atonement and utilize its power; the scriptures call these stepping-stones "the doctrine of Christ," or more simply "the gospel" (see 2 Nephi 31:21; Jacob 7:6). "This is the way; and there is none other way nor name given under heaven whereby man can be saved in the kingdom of God. And now, behold, *this is the doctrine of Christ*" (2 Nephi 31:21; emphasis added).

The doctrine of Christ is described concisely in 2 Nephi 31 (see also 3 Nephi 11) and even more concisely in the Fourth Article of Faith. It entails faith, repentance, covenant making (in particular, baptism), receiving the gift of the Holy Ghost, and enduring to the end of this life.

*Faith.* One of our most acute challenges on this earth is to learn to trust that Jesus lived and that His Atonement

## "The Dilemma: An Incomprehensible Atonement?"

was a real event which can have actual effect on our lives. As part of this process, we realize that we cannot comprehend everything. But Christ "comprehendeth all things" (D&C 88:41). The Savior understands the arithmetic of the infinite, and because He does, it is our test and challenge to trust that He knows and to keep moving forward and acting according to His will (see 1 Nephi 7:12). This process is what we call having "faith in Christ" (Enos 1:8).

The prophet Alma described this process with the analogy of a seed. He said that planting the word of God in our hearts is like planting a seed. Once the seed is planted, we cannot see it until after we have watered and nourished it. The seed then swells, sprouts, and starts to grow (see Alma 32:27–30). Alma went on to say that we should simply "begin to believe in the Son of God" and "plant this word in your hearts, and as it beginneth to swell even so nourish it by your faith. And behold, it will become a tree, springing up in you unto everlasting life. And then may God grant unto you that your burdens may be light, through the joy of his Son" (Alma 33:22–23). Trusting that Jesus's Atonement can free us from otherwise unbearable burdens is one of the great joys of the doctrine of Christ, of which faith is one of the founding principles.

*Repentance.* A natural result of a belief in Christ is a desire to repent or change; "therefore only unto him that has faith unto repentance is brought about the great and eternal plan of redemption" (Alma 34:16). We are placed here on earth in a "state to act according to [our own] wills and pleasures" (Alma 12:31). That means, among other things, that we must choose to repent. Repentance is our part of the equation, while forgiveness is God's. The "plan of redemption could not be brought about, only on conditions of repentance of men" (Alma 42:13). The act of receiving the cleansing and healing power of the Atonement must begin with our individual decision to repent.

*Making covenants.* As we exercise faith and change through repentance, we desire to bind ourselves to God to be called by the name of His Son, Jesus Christ (see 2 Nephi 31:13). The first covenant we make is baptism, "a witness and a testimony before God, and unto the people, that [we have] repented and received a remission of [our] sins" (3 Nephi 7:25). Entering this covenant shows that we will "serve him and keep his commandments," which leads Him to fulfill His promise that "he may pour out his Spirit more abundantly upon [us]" (Mosiah 18:10).

*The gift of the Holy Ghost.* Our willingness to have faith in Jesus Christ, to repent of our sins, and to make covenants that bind us to God opens us up to receive one of the greatest gifts that God has to offer on this earth—the Holy Ghost. The Holy Ghost, a member of the Godhead, can reveal all things to us and provide us with comfort (see John 14:26; 2 Nephi 32:5; D&C 20:28). But with regard to the power of the Atonement, one of the most stunning parts that the gift of the Holy Ghost plays takes place after we repent and are baptized by water: "Then cometh a remission of your sins by fire and by the Holy Ghost" (2 Nephi 31:17). There could not be any greater blessing than to have our sins burned away by the fire that the Holy Ghost represents. The peace and joy which follow this

## "The Dilemma: An Incomprehensible Atonement?"

cleansing power help us to understand the immediate and powerful effects of the Atonement of Christ.

### OUR ACTIONS

If recognizing the technical processes of the Atonement is all that we needed for salvation, then one would expect that characters such as Laman and Lemuel, or even Lucifer, would be assured of salvation because they knew of Christ and of what He did. Many people think that getting to know Jesus Christ is only a cognitive process, while in other matters they recognize the necessity both of knowing the facts about a particular process and of knowing the process through experience. Likewise, the scriptures promise that "if any man will do his will, he shall know of the doctrine, whether it be of God" (John 7:17). Three foundational actions will lead us to know the doctrine of Christ and will therefore help us gain access to the power of the Atonement: reading the scriptures, praying, and obeying the commandments.

*Reading the scriptures.* The simplest way for us to begin to understand Jesus Christ and His Atonement is by reading and studying what has been written about Him in scripture. We were not on the earth during Christ's mortal ministry, so we read and study the words of prophets who did live with Him and who have seen Him. The scriptures become an invaluable and consistent resource in our journey to "press forward, feasting upon the word of Christ" (2 Nephi 31:20). As John explained, we should "search the scriptures . . . [because] they are they which testify of [Christ]" (John

5:39). Our efforts to "lay hold upon the word of God . . . [will] divide asunder all the cunning and the snares and the wiles of the devil, and lead the man of Christ in a strait and narrow course" (Helaman 3:29).

*Praying.* We pray to our Heavenly Father in the name of Jesus Christ. We use this pattern because while we go to our Father in Heaven to ask for forgiveness, it is granted according to His will through the Atonement of His Son (see Mosiah 4:10). Enos knew that just wishing that his sins would be forgiven would not bring about absolution; instead, he needed to pray and use his agency to ask for that forgiveness (see Enos 1:4). Through prayer we gain access to the doors of heaven—only Satan, who knows that prayer is a means by which we can reach God, would keep us from praying (see 2 Nephi 32:8–9). It is through prayer that our souls access God and find rest from the weight of sin. The Nephites during the time of Helaman understood this connection well, for "they did fast and pray oft . . . unto the filling their souls with joy and consolation, yea, even to the purifying and the sanctification of their hearts" (Helaman 3:35).

*Obeying the commandments.* In its simplest form, obedience entails doing what Heavenly Father has asked us to do. Heavenly Father most often asks us to do certain things by issuing commandments. "And when we obtain any blessing from God, it is by obedience to that law upon which it is predicated" (D&C 130:21). Choosing to obey God, or using our will to do the will of God, is what opens up to us a reservoir of blessings, of which foremost is the blessing of forgiveness through the Atonement. A person can gain more knowledge and intelligence in this

## "The Dilemma: An Incomprehensible Atonement?"

life, particularly of the Atonement, by choosing to obey the commandments God has given us (see D&C 130:19). "Blessed are they that do his commandments, that they may have right to the tree of life," or in other words, to Jesus Christ, the Savior (Revelation 22:14; see also 1 Nephi 11:9, 21–22). These are some of the fundamental tools given to us from a loving Heavenly Father to guide us in accessing the cleansing and healing power of the Atonement.

### "How Is It Done?"

We read the familiar story of Enos, son of the prophet Jacob, who wanted desperately to receive a remission of his sins. In response to his lengthy petition for forgiveness, Enos heard the voice of God declare, "Enos, thy sins are forgiven thee" (Enos 1:5). Enos was certainly grateful for the mercy of God through the Atonement of His Son, but he still wondered, "Lord, how is it done?" (Enos 1:7). How does the life and experience of one person, even God, provide forgiveness to someone else who has sinned? While the specifics of how God performed these acts were still incomprehensible to Enos, the process was explained to him. The Lord's response was, "Because of thy faith in Christ" (Enos 1:7–8). Enos learned that his acceptance of the doctrine of Christ led to a remission of his sins and to a comprehension of the process by which that remission took place.

Enos exercised his faith by asking for forgiveness. Repentance was evidenced in his "wrestl[ing]" and "soul hunger[ing]" (Enos 1:2, 4). His covenants were manifested by actions associated with the name of Christ, specifically prayer. And the Holy Ghost was his attendant through the process (see Enos 1:2, 4, 5, 10). Most of what we learn and comprehend in this life comes from our five senses—seeing, hearing, touching, smelling, and tasting. However, communication with and subsequent learning from the Holy Ghost involves a different sense.[8] The Holy Ghost may not be easily defined in the same terms we use to define our other five senses, but it is nevertheless as real and immutable as those senses.

An example from King Benjamin helps us to understand the part the Holy Ghost plays in utilizing the Atonement's power more effectively. The people of King Benjamin, upon hearing the word of God, became aware that they had sinned and that they absolutely needed the blessing of forgiveness. They "viewed themselves in their own carnal state, even less than the dust of the earth," and their prayer was, "O have mercy, and apply the atoning blood of Christ that we may receive forgiveness of our sins" (Mosiah 4:2). Like Enos, King Benjamin's people wanted the mercy of the Lord to allow the atoning blood of Jesus Christ to be effective personally and immediately. That atoning forgiveness came through the Holy Ghost: "After they had spoken these words the Spirit of the Lord came upon them, and they were filled with joy, having received a remission of their sins, and having peace of conscience" (Mosiah 4:3). They had been forgiven through the Holy Ghost, and their evidence of forgiveness was the peace and joy that accompanied the remission of their sins.

The Atonement of Jesus Christ makes forgiveness of sin possible. But it is the Holy Ghost, the third member of the Godhead, who provides the activating and cleansing

## "The Dilemma: An Incomprehensible Atonement?"

power of the Atonement for each individual. The same means by which the Atonement was applied to each of King Benjamin's people is the same means by which it is applied to each of us. In Elder Henry B. Eyring's words, "If you have felt the influence of the Spirit this day, . . . you may take it as evidence that the Atonement is working in your life."[9]

Is the Atonement incomprehensible? In one sense, it is incomprehensible because it is infinite in nature; it is all-inclusive (sufficient for all of the sins, inadequacies, and physical deaths of men); and performed by God. All these aspects of the Atonement cannot be intimately or comprehensively understood in this mortal life. What we can understand now are the doctrines, the tools, and the process needed to access the healing and cleansing effects of the Atonement. Though we may not yet be like God, the Atonement and its attendant blessings are real and available now through the power of the Holy Ghost (see D&C 59:23).

### NOTES

1. Joseph Smith, *History of the Church of Jesus Christ of Latter-day Saints*, ed. B. H. Roberts, 2nd ed. rev. (Salt Lake City: Deseret Book, 1980), 3:30.
2. The scriptures speak of the "unpardonable sin" (Jacob 7:19; Alma 39:6) in which a person has sinned severely against the Holy Ghost. The scriptures teach that these few individuals will be "the only ones who shall not be redeemed in the due time of the Lord" to a kingdom of glory (D&C 76:38; see also D&C 76:32–38; Hebrews 6:4–6;

Joseph Smith, *Teachings of the Prophet Joseph Smith*, comp. Joseph Fielding Smith [Salt Lake City: Deseret Book, 1976], 358).

3. A similar discussion on this subject was offered by Stephen E. Robinson in *Believing Christ* (Salt Lake City: Deseret Book, 1992), 26.
4. For those who murder there is no forgiveness in this life. After this life and after they have suffered for their sin in hell, it is possible for them to receive redemption in the telestial world, but they cannot receive the exaltation of the celestial world (see D&C 76:81–86; D&C 138:58–59; Alma 5:21; Boyd K. Packer, "The Brilliant Morning of Forgiveness," *Ensign*, November 1995, 18; Smith, *Teachings of the Prophet Joseph Smith*, 339).
5. James E. Talmage, *Jesus the Christ* (Salt Lake City: Deseret Book, 1974), 569.
6. Bruce R. McConkie, "The Purifying Power of Gethsemane," *Ensign*, May 1985, 10.
7. Henry B. Eyring, "Spiritual Preparedness: Start Early and Be Steady," *Ensign*, November 2005, 38.
8. Boyd K. Packer, "Revelation in a Changing World," *Ensign*, November 1989; see also Richard G. Scott, "Helping Others to Be Spiritually Led," in *Doctrine and Covenants and Church History Symposium, 11–13 August 1998* (Salt Lake City: The Church of Jesus Christ of Latter-day Saints, 1998), 2.
9. Henry B. Eyring, "Gifts of the Spirit for Hard Times," *CES Fireside for Young Adults*, September 10, 2006, Brigham Young University.

DANA M. PIKE

# JESUS, THE GREAT SHEPHERD-KING

"The Lord is my shepherd; I shall not want. He maketh me to lie down in green pastures: he leadeth me beside the still waters" (Psalm 23:1–2). So begins one of the most beloved psalms and best-known biblical passages mentioning a shepherd. Shepherd imagery is utilized in scripture to depict three important aspects of Jesus's identity and mission: His roles as Savior, King, and Jehovah, the God of Israel. Of these three, His role as compassionate Savior, devoted to protecting and saving the flock of God, is the aspect of shepherd symbolism that typically comes to mind. Less well known, but equally important, is the royal dimension of the title "Shepherd." This study highlights both of these facets of shepherd symbolism associated with Jesus, giving extra emphasis to the royal

---

Dana M. Pike is a professor of ancient scripture at Brigham Young University.

one. Jesus's claim to be the Good Shepherd of Israel was also an unequivocal claim to His contemporaries that He was Jehovah, the God of Israel. A brief review of ancient shepherds' duties and of the figurative use of shepherds and sheep to refer to deities and humans in ancient Near Eastern texts, including the Bible, provides a context in which to consider Jesus as the great and divine Shepherd-King.

## SHEPHERDS AND SHEEP IN THE ANCIENT NEAR EAST[1]

Psalm 23 is not only a beautifully lyric expression of sincere convictions about Jehovah's love and protection; it also provides valuable insight into the work and attributes of real shepherds in ancient Israel. By culling information from this and other biblical passages, it is possible to obtain a good overview of the duties of ancient shepherds. As one scholar has observed: "Shepherding was one of man's earliest occupations. Flocks and herds, always a prominent feature in Palestine and other Near Eastern societies, consisted specifically of cows, sheep, and goats, but could also include horses, asses, and camels; the principal animal, however, owing to size, abundance, and usefulness, was the sheep."[2]

By day, a shepherd's duties consisted of leading his or her flock to food and water and protecting the sheep from wild animals and thieves. At night, shepherds often led their sheep into a cave or a "fold," a minicorral often built against the side of a hill, to keep the sheep from straying and to protect them from danger. Quality shepherds were

## "JESUS, THE GREAT SHEPHERD-KING"

thus dedicated, hardworking, compassionate leaders who provided for and protected and guided their flocks. Keeping a flock together was essential to accomplishing this mission.

### SHEPHERDS AND SHEEP IN SCRIPTURE

Terminology for sheep in the Hebrew Bible (what Christians call the Old Testament) is varied and somewhat overlapping. The words *ṣōʾn* and *śeh* designate "flocks," which can consist of both sheep and goats, but are often rendered as just "sheep," and *śeh* many times designates a "lamb" (e.g., Genesis 21:27; 22:7; Leviticus 5:7; Nehemiah 3:1).[3] The word *ʿēder* also refers to a "flock" of sheep and goats but could also be used for a herd of cattle.[4] The Hebrew word *kebeś* means "young sheep" and is also often translated "lamb" (e.g., Exodus 12:5; 29:38).[5] Only occasionally attested is *ṭĕlāʾ*, which also means "lamb."[6] More specifically, *ʾayil* is a "ram" (e. g., Isaiah 1:11), *rāḥēl* is a "ewe" (e. g., Isaiah 53:7), and *gĕdî* is a "kid," whether sheep or goat (e. g., Exodus 34:26).[7] Finally, the words *nōqēd* (e. g., Amos 1:1) and, more commonly, *rōʿeh* (e. g., Psalm 23:1) translate as "shepherd."[8]

The usual word for "sheep" in the Greek New Testament is *probaton*.[9] A "flock (of sheep)" is designated by the terms *poimnē* and *poimnion*.[10] The most commonly attested word for "lamb" is *arnon* (it also can indicate "ram" or "sheep"); *amnos* and *arēn* also occur with the same meaning.[11] "Shepherd," someone who tends or pastures (*poimainō*) the herd, is *poimēn*.[12]

## Celebrating Easter

There are many scripture passages in which real-life sheep and shepherds are mentioned. Some well-known biblical characters had flocks and worked as shepherds for at least part of their lives, including Abraham, Lot, Rachel, Jacob, Moses, and David. Two examples must suffice. Upon arriving in Haran, Jacob spoke with shepherds. "And while he yet spake with them, Rachel came with her father's sheep [ṣōʾn]: for she kept [rōʿāh, shepherded or pastured] them." Jacob, wanting to make a good first impression on his cousin Rachel, whose name means "ewe," "went near, and rolled the stone from the well's mouth, and watered the flock [ṣōʾn] of Laban his mother's brother" (Genesis 29:9–10). In one of several biblical passages mentioning David and sheep, David drew on his shepherding experience to present himself as capable of fighting Goliath, "And David said unto Saul, Thy servant kept [rōʿeh, "shepherded"] his father's sheep [ṣōʾn], and there came a lion, and a bear, and took a lamb [śeh] out of the flock: . . . and [I] delivered it out of his mouth. . . . Thy servant slew both the lion and the bear" (1 Samuel 17:34–36). Much later in David's life, the Lord reminded him "I took thee from the sheepcote, from following the sheep [ṣōʾn], to be ruler over my people, over Israel" (2 Samuel 7:8).

Sheep figure in a number of other biblical passages. For example, Abel "was a keeper [rōʿeh] of sheep [ṣōʾn]" (Genesis 4:2). At least one lamb [kebeś] was sacrificed every morning and every evening on the altar in front of the Israelite tabernacle (see Numbers 28:3–4; Exodus 29:39) and later at the temple in Jerusalem. The Bible recounts laws regulating the punishment for stealing or killing someone's sheep [śeh] and other animals (see Exodus 22).

## "JESUS, THE GREAT SHEPHERD-KING"

The counsel of the wise in ancient Israel was to "be thou diligent to know the state of thy flocks [ṣōʾn], and look well to thy herds" (Proverbs 27:23). Centuries later, Jesus referred to real sheep (to make a point about people) when he said, "What man of you, having an hundred sheep [*probaton*], if he lose one of them, doth not leave the ninety and nine in the wilderness, and go after that which is lost, until he find it?" (Luke 15:4). On another continent, Alma drew upon people's experience with sheep to support a religious point he was making: "For what shepherd is there among you having many sheep doth not watch over them, that the wolves enter not and devour his flock?" (Alma 5:59).

The commonness of shepherding in the ancient Near East, including ancient Israel, helps explain why shepherds and sheep became such regular and productive metaphors in scripture. Human rulers and God are referred to as shepherds, and people are referred to as sheep. This metaphor is productive because people have needs and challenges similar to sheep. The following sampling of the many pertinent scripture passages demonstrates the use of this imagery.[13]

*Human leaders as shepherds.* Toward the end of Moses's prophetic ministry, he requested that the Lord "set a man over the congregation [of Israel]. . . . which may lead them out, and which may bring them in; that the congregation of the Lord be not as sheep [ṣōʾn] which have no shepherd [rōʿeh]" (Numbers 27:16–17). Joshua was the shepherd-leader Jehovah chose to succeed Moses. Centuries later, through Isaiah the Lord prophesied of the future Persian king Cyrus II (538–530), stating that, "He is my shepherd [rōʿeh]" (Isaiah 44:28). After conquering the Babylonian empire, Cyrus allowed the Babylonian exiles, including many Jews, to return to their homelands, thus physically gathering some of these scattered Israelite "sheep." After His Resurrection, Jesus recommissioned Peter in his role as apostolic leader to "Feed my [Jesus's] lambs [*arnion*].... Feed my sheep [*probaton*]" (John 21:15–17).

*The Lord as shepherd.* Since Latter-day Saints understand that Jehovah and Jesus are the same being,[14] passages in both the Old and New Testaments are cited here to show the range of scriptures in which shepherd imagery is associated with the Lord. One passage usually missed by readers of the King James Version (KJV) is Genesis 48:15: "And he [Jacob] blessed Joseph, and said, God, before whom my fathers Abraham and Isaac did walk, the God which fed me all my life long unto this day." The Hebrew word rendered "fed" in the KJV is the participle *hārōʻeh*, which literally means "the one who shepherds or pastures, shepherd." Thus the New Revised Standard Version (NRSV) translates the last phrase in Genesis 48:15 as "the God who has been my shepherd all my life to this day."[15] Genesis 49:24 preserves another reference to Jehovah as a shepherd. In Jacob's blessing of Joseph, Jehovah is referred to as "the mighty God of Jacob; (from thence is the shepherd [*rōʻeh*], the stone of Israel)" (KJV, Genesis 49:24), or as rendered in the NRSV, "by the hands of the Mighty One of Jacob, by the name of the Shepherd, the Rock of Israel."[16] "Shepherd" and "Stone/Rock" are titles for Jehovah/Jesus.

Several biblical psalms contain passages praising Jehovah as a shepherd. For example, "The Lord is my shepherd [*rōʻeh*].... He maketh me to lie down in green

## "Jesus, the Great Shepherd-King"

pastures: he leadeth me beside the still waters" (Psalm 23:1–2); "[God] made his own people to go forth like sheep [$ṣō'n$], and guided them in the wilderness like a flock [$'ēder$]" (Psalm 78:52); and "Give ear, O Shepherd of Israel, thou that leadest Joseph like a flock [$'ēder$]" (Psalm 80:1). Similarly, Jehovah, referring to Himself, prophesied through Jeremiah that in the latter-days, "He that scattered Israel will gather him, and keep him, as a shepherd [$rō'eh$] doth his flock [$'ēder$]" (Jeremiah 31:10).[17]

What is lost in translation is that the expression "the LORD," in all capitals, renders the Hebrew divine name YHWH, or Jehovah.[18] Therefore, to say with the Psalmist, "The LORD is my shepherd," is the same as saying "Jehovah is my shepherd," which can be theologically rendered as "Jesus is my shepherd." Jesus proclaimed during His mortal ministry that He was "the good shepherd [$poimēn$]" (John 10:14), thus making a specific identification: He and Jehovah were the same being, the same Shepherd.

Passages in the New Testament in which Jesus refers to Himself or is referred to by others as a shepherd include Jesus's reference to Himself as the Judge of the world before whom "shall be gathered all nations: and he shall separate them one from another, as a shepherd [$poimēn$] divideth his sheep [$probaton$] from the goats" (Matthew 25:32); Jesus's application of the prophecy in Zechariah 13:9 to Himself as He headed to Gethsemane, "For it is written, I will smite the shepherd [$poimēn$], and the sheep [$probaton$] shall be scattered" (Mark 14:27);[19] "I am the good shepherd [$poimēn$]" (John 10:14); "our Lord Jesus, that great shepherd [$poimēn$] of the sheep [$probaton$]" (Hebrews 13:20); "the Shepherd [$poimēn$] and Bishop of your souls" (1 Peter 2:25); "and when the chief Shepherd [*archipoimēn*] shall appear" (1 Peter 5:4). Restoration scripture preserves similar usage, as illustrated by these two passages: "Their Redeemer, and their great and true shepherd" (Helaman 15:13) and "I am the good shepherd, and the stone of Israel" (D&C 50:44; compare Genesis 49:24).

These passages demonstrate how the use of "shepherd" as a title for Jehovah or Jesus was an appropriate expression of the intersection between the roles of a human shepherd—leading, protecting, providing for a flock—and Jesus's role as Savior of God's children.

*People as sheep in scripture.* Five of the many passages in the Old Testament in which people are metaphorically referred to as sheep are: "I saw all Israel scattered upon the hills, as sheep [*ṣōʾn*] that have not a shepherd [*rōʿeh*]" (1 Kings 22:17); "we are his people, and the sheep [*ṣōʾn*] of his pasture" (Psalm 100:3); "all we like sheep [*ṣōʾn*] have gone astray" (Isaiah 53:6); "Israel is a scattered sheep [*śeh*]" (Jeremiah 50:17); and "therefore they went their way as a flock [*ṣōʾn*], they were troubled, because there was no shepherd [*rōʿeh*]" (Zechariah 10:2).[20]

The authors of the New Testament Gospel accounts report that Jesus often employed sheep imagery in reference to people. The following verses illustrate this: "Beware of false prophets, which come to you in sheep's [*probaton*] clothing, but inwardly they are ravening wolves" (Matthew 7:15); "And before him shall be gathered all nations: and he shall separate them one from another, as a shepherd [*poimēn*] divideth his sheep [*probaton*] from the goats" (Matthew 25:32); "Fear not, little flock [*poimnion*]" (Luke

12:32); "He saith to him again the second time, Simon, son of Jonas, lovest thou me? . . . Feed my sheep [*probaton*]" (John 21:16). Jesus's audiences would have surely recognized the Old Testament roots of His figurative use of sheep to represent people.[21]

Other scriptural examples of such use include Paul's prophecy that "grievous wolves enter in among you [Christians], not sparing the flock [*poimnion*]" (Acts 20:29) and Abinadi's prophecy that Noah's priests would be "smitten on every hand, and shall be driven and scattered to and fro, even as a wild flock is driven by wild and ferocious beasts" (Mosiah 17:17).[22]

*The Lord's flock consists of His covenant people.* In reviewing the many passages of scripture in which sheep and shepherds are employed as metaphors, it is clear that Jesus and His prophets use the symbol of a flock of sheep to designate the Lord's covenant followers. But it is equally clear that there are multiple flocks of people in the world. All do not choose to be part of the same flock. Thus, for example, "Jesus answered [some Jewish leaders and said] . . . the works that I do in my Father's name, they bear witness of me. But ye believe not, because ye are not of my sheep [*probaton*], as I said unto you" (John 10:25–26; see also John 10:4, 16; Mosiah 26:21). And as Alma explicitly stated, "If ye will not hearken unto the voice of the good shepherd, . . . ye are not the sheep of the good shepherd; . . . the devil is your shepherd, and ye are of his fold" (Alma 5:38–39; see also Alma 5:60; Helaman 5:13). Thus, the relationship between the true Shepherd and His flock represents a covenant relationship between Jesus and those who follow His lead.[23]

*John 10: Jesus is the door to the sheepfold and the Good Shepherd.* During the last autumn of His life, six months before His crucifixion, Jesus was in Jerusalem at the Feast of Tabernacles (John 7:10–10:21). The events narrated at the end of John 9, in which Jesus spoke with some Jewish leaders following His healing of a man born blind (9:1–41), continue into John 10.[24] At this point, Jesus told these Jewish leaders one parable that contained two instances of sheep imagery: "Verily, verily, I say unto you, He that entereth not by the door into the sheepfold, but climbeth up some other way, the same is a thief and a robber. But he that entereth in by the door is the shepherd [*poimēn*] of the sheep [*probaton*] . . . and he calleth his own sheep [*probaton*] by name, and leadeth them out . . . and the sheep [*probaton*] follow him: for they know his voice. . . . This parable spake Jesus unto them: but they understood not . . . Then said Jesus unto them . . . I am the door of the sheep [*probaton*] . . . I am the door: by me if any man enter in, he shall be saved, and shall go in and out, and find pasture" (John 10:1–10).[25]

Drawing on the commonplace image of a shepherd with sheep in a sheepfold, Jesus specifically identified Himself as "the door," the means by which the flock entered the fold for protection. The fold can be metaphorically understood to represent Jesus's covenant followers on earth and, ultimately, the heavenly fold of the exalted.[26] Jesus thus emphasized the exclusive nature of His role as Redeemer. No one can enter into the Father's presence except "through" Jesus. There is no other "door." As He later taught His Apostles, "I am the way, the truth, and

## "JESUS, THE GREAT SHEPHERD-KING"

the life: no man cometh unto the Father, but by me" (John 14:6).

Having made this point, Jesus highlighted a second use of sheep imagery in the parable He taught the Jewish leaders in Jerusalem: "I am the good shepherd [*poimēn*]: the good shepherd [*poimēn*] giveth his life for the sheep. But he that is an hireling, and not the shepherd [*poimēn*] ... seeth the wolf coming, and leaveth the sheep [*probaton*], and fleeth: and the wolf ... scattereth the sheep [*probaton*] ... I am the good shepherd [*poimēn*], and know my sheep [literally, "know my own"], and am known of mine ... and I lay down my life for the sheep [*probaton*]. And other sheep [*probaton*] I have, which are not of this fold ... they shall hear my voice; and there shall be one fold [*poimnē*], and one shepherd [*poimēn*]" (John 10:11–16).

Jesus's devotion to His "sheep" as He taught here is a public announcement of His forthcoming sacrifice. His reference to Himself as the protecting and sacrificing "good Shepherd" motivated by compassion for His flock drew upon a shepherd's real-life duties. This correlation is further strengthened when other biblical passages are considered, such as, "He [Jehovah] shall feed his flock [*ʿēder*] like a shepherd [*rōʿeh*]: he shall gather the lambs [*ṭĕlāʾ*] with his arm, and carry them in his bosom, and shall gently lead those that are with young" (Isaiah 40:11).

Jesus, however, was teaching far more on that occasion in Jerusalem than that He was a devoted and compassionate leader of God's "sheep." Seeing only this aspect of Jesus's identity as Shepherd in John 10:11–16 is to miss a powerfully pointed aspect of His message to the Jewish leaders, who would have found nothing offensive or inflammatory in Jesus's claims to be a compassionate person who was willing to give up His life. It was the royal and divine dimensions of the symbolism of the title "Shepherd" that was so troublesome to them. The inherent implication that as the good Shepherd He was Jehovah, their God, has already been explicated. The association of the title "shepherd" with kings will now be set forth.

## THE TITLE "SHEPHERD" IN NONBIBLICAL ANCIENT NEAR EASTERN TEXTS[27]

In addition to the figurative use of shepherd and sheep in the Bible and other scriptures (reviewed above), such use is also documented in other ancient Near Eastern texts during the two millennia prior to Jesus's mortal ministry. The following passages, extracted from ancient Mesopotamian (Sumerian, Babylonian, and Assyrian)[28] and Egyptian texts, illustrate that the use of the title "shepherd" in reference to deities and kings was an age-old tradition with which people in the ancient Near East were well acquainted.[29]

*Deities.* Marduk, the chief deity of Babylonia, is referred to in the Babylonian "Epic of Creation" (*Enuma elish*) as a "faithful shepherd,"[30] and at one point other deities proclaim, "He [Marduk] shall be the shepherd of the black-headed folk [humans], his creatures."[31] Elsewhere, a prayer includes the request, "May he [Marduk] shepherd human beings like sheep!"[32] Shamash, the Babylonian sun god and god of justice, is proclaimed the "shepherd of the lower [mortal] world, guardian of the upper."[33] An unnamed Mesopotamian deity is described in one text as "the god of the man, the shepherd who seeks pasture for the man."[34] The Egyptian god Re is described as a "Valiant shepherd who drives his flock, / Their refuge, made to sustain them."[35]

Many ancient Near Eastern personal names, including those of Israelites, were compounds that included a divine name.[36] Elijah, for example, means "My-God-is-Jehovah." Examples of pertinent Mesopotamian personal names include, in translation, "Shamash-is-my-shepherd," "Adad-is-my-shepherd," and "My-Lord-is-(my-) Shepherd."[37]

*Kings*. As earthly representatives of their deities, ancient Near Eastern kings were often described as shepherds of the people they ruled. Examples of royal claims employing shepherd and sheep imagery are cited here in chronological order.

- Gudea (Sumerian *ensi*; 2144–2124 BC) was a "shepherd who leads the people with a good religious hand."[38]
- Lipit-Ishtar (Isin; 1934–1924 BC): "Lipit-Ishtar, the wise shepherd, whose name has been pronounced by the god Nunamnir."[39]
- Hammurabi (Babylonia, 1792–1750 BC): "I am Hammurabi, the shepherd, selected by the god Enlil, he who heaps high abundance and plenty . . . [the one] who gathers together the scattered peoples."[40] "I provided perpetual water for the land . . . [and] gathered the scattered peoples. . . . In abundance and plenty I shepherded them."[41]

- Amenhotep III (Egypt; 1411–1374 BC): "the good shepherd, vigilant for all people."[42]
- Seti I (Egypt; 1313–1292 BC): "the good shepherd, who preserves his soldiers alive."[43]
- Merneptah (Egypt; 1225–1215 BC): "I am the ruler who shepherds you."[44]
- Merodach-baladan I (Babylonia; 1171–1159 BC): "[I am] the shepherd who collects the dispersed (people)."[45]
- Adadnirari III (Assyria; 810–783 BC): "unrivalled king, wonderful shepherd . . . whose shepherdship the great gods have made pleasing to the people of Assyria."[46]
- Esarhaddon (Assyria; 680–669 BC): "the true shepherd, favorite of the great gods."[47]
- Assurbanipal (Assyria; 668–627 BC): "those peoples which Ashur, Ishtar and the (other) great gods had given to me to be their shepherd and had entrusted into my hands."[48]
- Nabopolassar (Babylonia; 625–605 BC): "the king of justice, the shepherd called by Marduk."[49]
- Nebuchadnezzar II (Babylonia; 604–562 BC): "Marduk . . . gave me the shepherdship of the country and the people," and "the loyal shepherd, the one permanently selected by Marduk."[50]

In addition to such royal claims, the connection between royalty and shepherd symbolism occurs in ancient Egypt "in the widespread [artistic depictions] of the simple shepherd's crook as an insignia of kings, princes, and chieftains. The instrument symbolized the ruler's power

## "Jesus, the Great Shepherd-King"

and eminence, and especially the nature of his rule, the king's obligation to maintain order and justice [*maʿat*] in the land."[51]

As is evident from these examples selected from the many that could have been cited, the imagery and title of "shepherd" was commonly used to represent divine and human royal leadership in the ancient Near East for two millennia before Jesus's ministry. Kings employed it to illustrate their divine sanction to rule, their ability to provide and care for their subjects, and their power to protect their people from enemies. This title "Shepherd" and the attributes it conveys overlap with the shepherd imagery preserved in the Bible and must be considered in connection with John 10. Jesus claimed to be not only the door of the sheepfold but the Good Shepherd Himself. Understood in the cultural context of the ancient Near East, there was a *royal* dimension to Jesus's claim. He thus employed the image of shepherd to communicate His identity as the devoted and compassionate Savior *and* His identity as a King. This assertion is further borne out by prophecy in the Old Testament, particularly in the book of Ezekiel.

### EZEKIEL 34 AND 37: THE MESSIANIC SHEPHERD-KING

The first half of the book of Ezekiel contains a series of prophecies of judgment and destruction against the Israelites in the kingdom of Judah (in its last gasp of existence before 586 BC) and against neighboring nations. This is followed by a series of prophecies about the future restoration of the house of Israel, including these statements in chapter 34 in which shepherds and sheep symbolize the leaders and people of Israel:

> Woe be to the shepherds [*rōʿeh*] of Israel that do feed themselves! should not the shepherds [*rōʿeh*] feed [*yirʿû*, shepherd or pasture] the flocks [*ṣōʾn*]? . . .
>
> They [the people/"sheep"] were scattered, because there is no shepherd [*rōʿeh*]: and they became meat to all the beasts of the field, when they were scattered.
>
> My sheep [*ṣōʾn*] wandered through all the mountains, and upon every high hill: yea, my flock [*ṣōʾn*] was scattered upon all the face of the earth, and none did search or seek after them. . . .
>
> As a shepherd [*rōʿeh*] seeketh out his flock [*ʿēder*] . . . will I [Jehovah] seek out my sheep [*ṣōʾn*]. . . .
>
> I will feed [*ʾerʿeh*, shepherd or pasture] them in a good pasture. . . . and I will cause them to lie down. . . .
>
> And they shall no more be a prey. . . .
>
> And I will set up one shepherd [*rōʿeh*] over them, and he shall feed [*rāʿāh*, shepherd or pasture] them, even my servant David; he shall feed [*yirʿeh*, shepherd or pasture] them, and he shall be their shepherd [*rōʿeh*]. . . .
>
> My servant David a prince among them. . . .
>
> Ye my flock [*ṣōʾn*], the flock [*ṣōʾn*] of my pasture, are men, and I am your God, saith the Lord God. (Ezekiel 34:2, 5–6, 12, 14, 22–24, 31)[52]

This notion of a royal servant, "David," who will gather and shepherd the lost sheep of Israel is prophesied again a few chapters later, in Ezekiel 37: "And David my servant shall be king over them; and they all shall have one

76

"Jesus, the Great Shepherd-King"

shepherd [*rōʿeh*]" (v. 24). Given that King David died about four centuries before Ezekiel prophesied, to whom do these prophecies of a future Davidic Shepherd-King refer? Most Christians, and certainly Latter-day Saints, accept these as messianic prophecies about the future deliverer of Israel, of whom the shepherd-turned-king David was a tragically flawed "type." They foretell that Jesus, as the "son [or descendant] of David," will gather the flock of covenant Israel and reign with justice as King of kings. These prophecies will be most fully realized during the Millennium, when the kingdom of God is fully established on this earth.[53]

## JESUS, THE GREAT SHEPHERD-KING

The passages reviewed above abundantly illustrate that shepherd symbolism was inextricably associated with ancient Near Eastern kings and their claims about themselves. This evidence is consistently represented throughout many centuries, and is contained in some important messianic prophecies in Israelite scripture (see Ezekiel 34; 37).

So Jesus's proclamation to Jewish leaders in Jerusalem that He was the Good Shepherd relayed three important aspects of His identity. He *was* claiming to be a devoted and compassionate leader who was willing to sacrifice His life for His sheep. He was *also* claiming to be a king, a *royal* shepherd. In this context, Jesus was specifically claiming to be the "son of David," the royal Messiah come in fulfillment of prophecy. Furthermore, His use of shepherd imagery conveyed that He was Jehovah, their God, come in the flesh.

Both the widely accepted royal nature of the title "shepherd" and the specific messianic passages in Ezekiel must have come quickly and powerfully to the minds of those who heard Jesus's proclamation in Jerusalem. The message of the imagery He employed in relation to Himself was not lost on His audience. If we miss the royal and divine dimensions of the symbolism in Jesus's teaching on that occasion, we miss the full and clear measure of His self-declaration. Referring to Himself as the Good Shepherd of Israel was an open announcement by Jesus that He was Jehovah, the Messiah, the King of Israel. This helps explain why "many of them said, he hath a devil, and is mad" (John 10:20), and why He was eventually charged with blasphemy, since most Jews at that time did not believe Jehovah would come in the flesh, did not understand that their Messiah and Jehovah were the same being, and did not accept Jesus's claims, implicit and explicit, that He was their divine and royal Messiah.[54]

## CONCLUSION

A wonderfully illustrative passage in Revelation 7 provides a fitting conclusion to this study. The Apostle John recounts that as he gazed in vision upon the heavenly throne room he saw "a great multitude . . . of all nations, and kindreds, and people, and tongues, [that] stood before the throne, and before the Lamb [*arnion*], clothed with white robes, and palms in their hands; And cried with a loud voice, saying, Salvation to our God which sitteth upon the throne, and unto the Lamb [*arnion*]" (Revelation

7:9–10). John learned the identification of these people from the angelic messenger who was conducting him through this vision. Notice how the imagery reviewed above—a Shepherd and His "sheep"—comes together to dramatically represent King Jesus and His redeeming accomplishment. John's escort said to him, "These are they who have . . . washed their robes and made them white in the blood of the Lamb [*arnion*] . . . they will hunger no more, and thirst no more . . . for the Lamb [*arnion*] at the center of the throne will be their shepherd [*poimainō*], and he will guide them to springs of the water of life" (NRSV, Revelation 7:13–17).[55]

From prophetic statements about Jehovah in the Old Testament to Jesus's teachings about Himself during His mortal ministry, from the additional witness of Restoration scripture to John's apocalyptic vision, Jehovah/Jesus is consistently represented as the great Shepherd-King who gathers, leads, provides, protects, and saves. He is worthy of all the praise His sanctified flock can render.[56]

NOTES

1. The Near East is essentially the same region more popularly known today as the Middle East.
2. Jack W. Vancil, "Sheep, Shepherd," in *Anchor Bible Dictionary*, ed. David N. Freedman (New York: Doubleday, 1992), 5:1187; hereafter *ABD*.
3. See *The Hebrew and Aramaic Lexicon of the Old Testament*, ed. Ludwig Koehler and Walter Baumgartner, rev. Walter Baumgartner and Johann Jakob Stamm, trans. and ed. M. E. J. Richardson (Brill: New York, 1994–2000), 992–93,

and 1310–11; hereafter *HALOT*. The masculine singular forms of all Hebrew words are cited in the body of the text because they are the lexical forms. Other grammatical forms are attested. *HALOT* provides further examples. This is not the place to discuss the impact of context on the use of these various terms, nor how the biblical text often augments the use of particular terms to help clarify the intended meaning. Further comments can be found under the pertinent entries in *Theological Dictionary of the Old Testament*, ed. G. Johannes Botterweck and Helmer Ringgren, trans. John T. Willis (Grand Rapids, MI: Eerdmans, 1974–).

4. See *HALOT*, 793.
5. See *HALOT*, 460. See also the variant *keśeb* (*HALOT*, 501). The KJV translation of Exodus 12:5 provides one illustration of the overlapping interplay between the use of these different terms: "Your lamb [*śeh*] shall be without blemish, a male of the first year: ye shall take it out from the sheep [*kĕbāśîm*], or from the goats."
6. See *HALOT*, 375.
7. See *HALOT*, 40, 1216, and 178.
8. See *HALOT*, 719–20; 1260–62. The word *rōʿeh* is a participle, derived from the verb *rʿh*, "to pasture" (*HALOT*, 1258–60).
9. The oldest extant manuscripts of the New Testament are in Greek, which was the language in which most, if not all, of the New Testament writings were originally composed.

For information on the Greek terms cited herein and their occurrence in the New Testament, see *Exegetical Dictionary of the New Testament*, ed. Horst Balz and

## "Jesus, the Great Shepherd-King"

Gerhard Schneider (Grand Rapids, MI: Eerdmans, 1990–1993); hereafter *EDNT*. For the Greek word *probaton*, see *EDNT*, 3:152–53.

10. See *EDNT*, 3:127–28.
11. See *EDNT*, 1:70–72.
12. See *EDNT*, 3:126–27.
13. Above and in the following comments only a few examples are given from the many scripture passages that could be cited, so as not to belabor the obvious. For further citations, see the Topical Guide under "Sheep," "Shepherd," and "Flock," and the summary accounts on the pertinent entries in *ABD* and *Eerdmans Dictionary of the Bible*, ed. David Noel Freedman (Grand Rapids, MI: Eerdmans, 2000).
14. This doctrinal perspective is well attested in both canonical scripture and latter-day prophetic statements. See, for example, the LDS Guide to the Scriptures (www.lds.org), s. v., "Jehovah" and "Jehovah is Christ."
15. Other modern English translations, such as the New Jewish Publication Society (NJPS) and the New International Version (NIV) render this phrase the same ("the God who has been my shepherd") as in the New Revised Standard Version (NRSV). See note "c" for Genesis 48:15 in the LDS edition of the KJV for a similar explanation of the Hebrew.
16. The KJV renders the phrase preserved in the Masoretic Text (the traditional Hebrew text) literally, even though it is hard to understand. Because this phrase is quite challenging, the NRSV translators chose to ignore the traditional vocalization. Their rendition of the Hebrew word "there" (KJV, "thence") as "name" is based on a

revocalization of the consonants in the Masoretic Text, influenced by the reading in the Syriac version of this verse. However, Nahum Sarna, *The JPS Torah Commentary: Genesis* (New York: Jewish Publication Society, 1989), 343, accepts the reading in the Masoretic Text, "there" (or "from there") as the best option, suggesting that Jacob "may have pointed heavenward" as he said this.

17. See also Isaiah 40:11 and Ezekiel 34:12, both of which are cited below.
18. For a discussion of this practice, see Dana M. Pike, "Biblical Hebrew Words You Already Know, and Why They are Important," *Religious Educator* 7, no. 3 (2006): 106–9.
19. For a non-LDS discussion of this passage and its relation to the important but challenging prophecy in Zechariah 13:7–9, see F. F. Bruce, *The New Testament Development of Old Testament Themes* (Grand Rapids, MI: Eerdmans, 1969), 100–14. Bruce's remarks are in a chapter he entitled "The Shepherd King," which I thank John W. Welch for sharing with me. The similarity between Bruce's chapter and the title of this study is due to the topic under examination, since I did not see Bruce's publication until after much of this paper was written and its title had been selected. See also Clay Alan Ham, *The Coming King and the Rejected Shepherd: Matthew's Reading of Zechariah's Messianic Hope* (Sheffield: Sheffield Phoenix, 2005).
20. Some other passages illustrating such usage include Numbers 27:17; 2 Samuel 24:17; Psalms 44:11, 12; 74:1; 119:176; Jeremiah 50:6, 17; and Micah 2:12.
21. Some other passages illustrating such usage include Matthew 9:36; 10:6, 16; and 15:24.

22. Some other passages illustrating such usage include Isaiah 63:11; 1 Peter 5:2, 3; Alma 5:60; Helaman 5:13; 3 Nephi 15:21, 24; 18:31; and D&C 6:34.
23. Victor L. Ludlow, *Principles and Practices of the Restored Gospel* (Salt Lake City: Deseret Book, 1992), 203, expressed it the other way around when he observed that "being the Good Shepherd and the appointed caretaker of God's children on earth, Christ is the administrator of God's covenants."
24. The chapter indication and summary at the beginning of John 10 interrupt the flow of the narrative. The "you" in John 10:1 links back to "them," the Jewish leaders (specifically Pharisees) to whom Jesus was speaking in John 9:40–41.
25. This is one of a few biblical passages that indicate that shepherds in ancient Israel *led* their flocks, rather than driving their flocks from behind (see also Psalms 23:2; contrast 2 Samuel 7:8). Many modern shepherds in the Middle East still practice this type of shepherding.
26. For further comment on this concept, see Bruce R. McConkie, *Doctrinal New Testament Commentary, Volume 1, The Gospels* (Salt Lake City: Bookcraft, 1974), 1:484.
27. The following passages, for the most part, are cited from standard collections of ancient Near Eastern texts in translation.
28. "Mesopotamia" is a term first used by the Greeks to designate the region now occupied by Iraq. The two major nations in Mesopotamia anciently were Assyria and Babylonia. Sumer was located in southern Mesopotamia.

29. As with the scriptures, only a few of the many examples that could be cited are included here. I have not included the Sumerian, Akkadian, or Egyptian terms in brackets, since this language is less well-known than Hebrew and Greek. Suffice it to say that Akkadian *rēʾû*, "shepherd," is cognate with Hebrew *rōʿeh*.
30. James B. Pritchard, ed., *Ancient Near Eastern Texts Relating to the Old Testament*, 3rd ed. (Princeton: Princeton University, 1969), 71; hereafter *ANET*.
31. *The Context of Scripture*, ed. William H. Hallo and K. Lawson Younger (New York: Brill, 1997–2002), 1:402 (text 1.112); hereafter *COS*.
32. *COS*, 1:469 (text 1.138).
33. *ANET*, 388.
34. Quoted in *The Assyrian Dictionary*, vol. 14/R. ed. Robert D. Biggs, and others (Chicago: Oriental Institute, 1999), 309; hereafter *CAD*.
35. *COS*, 1:44 (text 1.27).
36. These are known as theophoric names. For a discussion of this type of ancient name, see Dana M. Pike, "Names, Theophoric," *ADB*, 4:1018–19.
37. Quoted in *CAD*, 14:310. Such personal names, compounded with "shepherd" and the names of various deities are attested all over the ancient Near East. For references to such, see the citations of comparative evidence in *HALOT*, 1258–59.
38. As cited by Vancil, "Sheep, Shepherd," *ABD*, 5:1187.
39. *COS*, 2:411 (text 2.154).
40. *COS*, 2:336 (text 2.131).
41. *COS*, 2:257 (text 2.107B).
42. Quoted in *ABD*, 5:1189.

43. Quoted in *ABD*, 5:1189.
44. Quoted in *ABD*, 5:1189.
45. Quoted in *CAD*, 14:311.
46. *COS*, 2:275 (text 2.114E).
47. *ANET*, 289.
48. *ANET*, 298. See also, *COS*, 1:473: "May Shamash, king of heaven and earth, raise you [Assurbanipal] to shepherdship over the four regions!"
49. *COS*, 2:307. See also, "The shepherd who pleases Papnunanki" (*COS*, 2:308).
50. Both quotations from *COS*, 2:309.
51. *ABD*, 5:1188. See representative examples in James B. Pritchard, ed., *The Ancient Near East in Pictures Relating to the Old Testament*, 2nd ed. (Princeton: Princeton University Press,1969), pictures 379, 383, 545, 557 (the god Osiris).
52. For another passage in which delinquent shepherd-leaders are condemned, see Zechariah 11:15–17.
53. This is evident from the paradise-like content of the following verses (24–28). See also the comments of Bruce R. McConkie, *The Millennial Messiah: The Second Coming of the Son of Man* (Salt Lake City: Deseret, 1982), 606–8. For a new study of this topic, by a non-Latter-day Saint, see Youngs. Chae, *Jesus as the Eschatological Divinic Shepherd: Studies in the Old Testament, Second Temple Judaism, and in the Gospel of Matthew* (Tübigen: Mohr Siebeck, 2006).
54. Furthermore, most Jews believed their Messiah would be a human endowed with great powers, not the Son of God in the flesh.

55. This last quotation, Revelation 7:17, was taken from the NRSV. Compare the KJV, "For the Lamb which is in the midst of the throne shall feed them." Somewhat similarly to the situation in Genesis 48:15 (noted above), the KJV translators here rendered the Greek verb *poimanei* (from *poimaiño*, "to herd or shepherd") in Revelation 7:17 as the vague "feed," while many modern English translations, including the NRSV and the NIV, render it with more focus, but less grammatical accuracy, as "their shepherd."

56. I thank my research assistants Adam Anderson and Justin Soderquist for their help gathering source material for this article (much more than is included here!).

ERIC D. HUNTSMAN

# THE BREAD OF LIFE SERMON

> Whoso eateth my flesh, and drinketh my blood, hath eternal life; and I will raise him up at the last day. For my flesh is meat indeed, and my blood is drink indeed. He that eateth my flesh, and drinketh my blood, dwelleth in me, and I in him. As the living Father hath sent me, and I live by the Father: so he that eateth me, even he shall live by me. This is that bread which came down from heaven: not as your fathers did eat manna, and are dead: he that eateth of this bread shall live for ever. (John 6:54–58)

These concluding statements in Jesus's powerful and heavily symbolic Bread of Life discourse caused confusion, consternation, and even anger among many of its original hearers, both among the Jews and among some of Jesus's own disciples. The

---

Eric D. Huntsman is an assistant professor of ancient scripture at Brigham Young University.

discourse given in John 6:26–58 is the central of seven of Christ's discourses in John's Gospel that teach important truths about who Jesus is and what He does for mankind.[1] Thus, this sermon, along with the other discourses in John, focuses on Christology—understanding the person and the work of Jesus as the Messiah, or Anointed One.

Biblical scholarship has, for the most part, interpreted the discourse along one of three lines. One approach tends to focus on the sacramental aspect of the discourse, using the sacrament of the Lord's Supper to interpret it. A second approach interprets the sermon largely as a metaphor, seeing in the sermon a description of Jesus's role and the believer's response to Him. A third position does both, seeing the original discourse delivered by Jesus as primarily symbolic while acknowledging that John could well have intended the imagery to be applied to the sacrament.[2] These approaches echo the questions that Elder Bruce R. McConkie raised at the beginning of his own analysis of the discourse: "How do men eat the Lord's flesh and blood? Is this literal or figurative? Does it have reference to the sacrament of the Lord's Supper or to something else?"[3]

A sacramental approach to the Bread of Life sermon is particularly attractive since the Gospel of John strikingly omits any reference to the institution of the sacrament in its account of the Last Supper in John 13–14. Nevertheless, the discourse's focus on Christology was necessitated by the historical circumstances at the time of its delivery. Jesus's original audience consisted of several different groups: the crowd whose members had been present at or heard about the miraculous feeding of the five thousand (John

## "THE BREAD OF LIFE SERMON"

6:26–40), a specific group that John identifies as "the Jews" (vv. 41–59), and finally Jesus's followers, both a group of disciples and His innermost circle of the Twelve (vv. 60–71). Each of these groups misunderstood in some way either who Jesus was or what His mission was, allowing Jesus to adjust the focus of the discourse for each group. Therefore, the third approach to the sermon—considering it symbolic but recognizing its imagery in the ordinance of the sacrament—is particularly useful for understanding how Jesus's immediate audience responded to Him, which helps us better understand what we must believe about what He did for us by suffering and dying for the sins of the world. In the Easter season, this is particularly appropriate, since the imagery of eating Jesus's flesh and drinking His blood recalls to mind His suffering and death.

### THE PASSOVER SETTING AND THE PRECEDING MIRACLES

John establishes the setting of the discourse, "And the Passover, a feast of the Jews, was nigh" (v. 4), and consequently provides important interpretive hints. Unlike other Passovers in John, in this instance Jesus does not attend the festival in Jerusalem. Instead, He ascends a "mountain" (v. 3) in a locale that the synoptics identify as a wilderness (*erēmos topos*, KJV "desert place"), which strengthens the association of Jesus with the new Moses. It also provides imagery of deliverance and bread that makes Jesus's feeding the multitude in the wilderness so reminiscent of the Lord's sustaining the children of Israel while they were in the wilderness with Moses.[4] The

Passover setting establishes some of the fundamental symbolism necessary for understanding the Bread of Life discourse, including deliverance, the crossing of the sea, miraculous feedings in the wilderness, and the saving role of the Paschal Lamb. Although this episode does not take place in Jerusalem where the Passover was properly celebrated, it does associate this scene closely with the final Passover of Jesus's ministry.

Associating the two miracle stories of John 6—the feeding of the five thousand (John 6:5–15; parallels Matthew 14:13–21; Mark 6:33–44; Luke 9:11–17) and Jesus's walking on water (John 6:16–21; parallels Matthew 14:22–36; Mark 6:47–51)—with the Passover helps establish the imagery of the Bread of Life sermon. First, the miraculous, filling meal of bread and fish for the multitude re-creates the table fellowship of the Passover meal; Jesus extends the blessings of His meal to the thousands whom He fed, all the while hearkening back to Jehovah's provision of manna and flesh to the Israelites in the wilderness.[5] Jesus is established as the new Moses.

Second, Jesus walking on the water as told in John 6:16–21 continues the Passover imagery from the book of Exodus, recounting the crossing of the Red Sea; this miracle makes an important Christological statement, identifying Jesus directly with Jehovah and providing an important corrective to the contemporary messianic expectations encouraged by the record of the feeding of the five thousand. Whereas the feeding miracle could be interpreted too narrowly, as a sign that Jesus was only a messianic king, His walking on the water and miraculous completion of the sea voyage serves as a sign that He was

## "The Bread of Life Sermon"

far more. In the first verse of this pericope, John records, "When Jesus therefore perceived that they would come and take him by force, to make him a king, he departed again into a mountain himself alone" (v. 15). The crowd's desire to make Jesus a temporal ruler reflects many of the messianic expectations of the time, which, at least since the time of the Maccabees, have suffered an overly political interpretation which actually presented a false Christology of who the Messiah would be—a political ruler—and what He would do—deliver them from Herodian rule and Roman occupation.

Jesus's power over the water reveals, however, that He is far more than a great ruler or a worldly deliver. He is, in fact, King of Heaven and Earth, and, implicitly, their Creator. John emphasizes this fact by employing the formula "I Am" (Greek *egō eimi*) even more explicitly than do Matthew and Mark.[6] In John's substantially briefer account of Jesus's control of the raging sea and bringing His disciples safely to shore, He is manifested as the one exercising the power that the Hebrew Bible attributes to Jehovah alone (see Job 9:8, 38:16; Habakkuk 3:15).[7] Thus, in the Passover context of the Bread of Life sermon, Jesus's walking on the water reveals Him as both the one who created the deep and brought the Israelites through it. As Bertil Gärtner writes, "Just as the Lord ploughed a path for Israel through the sea, leading them to freedom from bondage, so Jesus, when he walks on the water, shows that as Messiah he has power over the seas."[8]

Celebrating Easter

WORDS TO THE MULTITUDE (6:22-40)

As noted, the Bread of Life sermon can be divided into three parts. In each part Jesus addresses a different target audience, each of which has misunderstood who Jesus is and what He came into the world to do. The first part begins with a narrative transition from the miracles that preceded the sermon in which the people (*ho ochlos*, which the KJV translates "the multitude") have followed Jesus and the disciples across the Sea of Galilee and found Him at Capernaum (John 6:22–25). This first part of the discourse, delivered to the multitude, consists of two distinct sections, a more general discussion of the Bread come down from heaven, which focuses on correcting the crowd's incorrect expectation of who the Messiah would be (6:26–34), and a specific pronouncement that Jesus Himself is the Bread of Life, which explains why Jesus came into the world (vv. 35–40).

In the first section, Jesus notes that the multitude have sought Him not because it has seen the miracles and recognized other divine signs of His identity but because it has eaten the bread which He had provided the previous day (v. 26). The manna that Israel had enjoyed under Moses came six days a week for forty years until it ceased after the last Passover Israel celebrated before coming into Canaan (see Joshua 5:10–12).[9] Because Moses had promised in Deuteronomy 18:15 that a prophet "like unto [him]" would come, the crowd expects the Messiah to perform the same miracles that Moses had, including providing manna. Intertestamental writings, for instance, confirm that a tradition arose that a second deliverer, the

## "The Bread of Life Sermon"

Messiah, would bring a new dispensation of manna at the opening of the new age as Moses, the first deliverer, had provided manna during the Exodus.[10]

Although Jesus avoided the multitude's attempt to make Him king the day before, the crowd's desire for more bread betrays a worldly conception of a Messiah whose primary purposes are not only to deliver them politically but also to provide for their temporal needs. Accordingly Jesus immediately tries to move the multitude away from the idea of manna and, in fact, even beyond His own miraculous feeding of the crowds the previous day. Recalling that the Mosaic manna quickly decayed and that even His own bread did not permanently satisfy the people's need for food, Jesus enjoins, "Labour not for the meat [*brōsin*, a generic word for "food"] which perisheth, but for that meat [*brōsin*] which endureth unto everlasting life, which the Son of man shall give unto you" (v. 27).

Joseph Smith's translation adds an important idea to the previous verse, "Ye seek me, *not because ye desire to keep my sayings*, neither because ye saw the miracles, but because ye did eat of the loaves and were filled" (Joseph Smith Translation, John 6:26; emphasis added). This helps explain why the multitude, subtly rebuked for its selfish expectation of the Messiah's mission, begins to realize its responsibility to respond in some way to Jesus in order to receive this imperishable food, and asks, "What shall we do, that we might work the works of God?" (John 6:28). Jesus responds, "This is the work of God, that ye believe on him whom he has sent" (v. 29). Instead, the crowd demands a sign and returns to the theme of bread, proclaiming, "Our fathers did eat manna in the desert; as it is written, he gave them bread from heaven to eat" (v. 31; see Psalm 78:24). To this Jesus replies, "Verily, verily, I say unto you, Moses gave you not that bread from heaven; but my Father giveth you the true bread from heaven" (v. 32). Besides qualifying that God, not Moses, gave the Israelites the manna that sustained them in the wilderness, Jesus's response focuses His audience on true bread, as opposed to perishable food that sustains life for only a day. While actual bread sustains physical life, both the bread and human life are temporal and perish. More important are what the manna during the Exodus and the loaves at the feeding of the five thousand represented.

Old Testament images of eating and drinking, wherein God's people eat His word (see Jeremiah 15:16; Exekiel 2:8, 3:1), specifically established food as a metaphor for spiritual sustenance.[11] The later Jewish understanding that manna represented the Torah, or Law,[12] is supported by Jesus's own words regarding bread and the word of God. Although John lacks an account of Jesus's temptation in the wilderness, the use of bread in the temptation accounts of the synoptics is illuminating (see Matthew 4:1–4; Luke 4:1–4). In them, Satan tests Jesus, encouraging Him to make bread out of stones, an act which, if performed, would have foreshadowed His turning water into wine or the multiplication of bread. Jesus's response is to quote part of Deuteronomy 8:3, which in full bears the Bread of Life sermon: "And he humbled thee, and suffered thee to hunger, and fed thee with manna, which thou knewest not, neither did thy fathers know; that he might make thee know that man doth not live by bread only, but by every word that proceedeth out of the mouth of the Lord doth

## "The Bread of Life Sermon"

man live." Therefore, as Moses had given spiritual food in the form of the Law, Jesus—the Son of Man—was offering true bread from heaven not merely to support physical life but also to support spiritual, everlasting life.

Because manna could represent the Torah in Moses's context, the multitude no doubt expects its question about working the works of God to be answered in terms of keeping the injunctions and ceremonies of the Law. As a result, the crowd may very well have misinterpreted Jesus's next saying, "For the bread of God is he which cometh down from heaven, and giveth life unto the world" (John 6:33). Although the Aramaic or Hebrew original is not preserved, the Greek for "he which cometh down" (*ho katabainōn*) is ambiguous because *ho katabainōn* can either be taken substantively as "*he* who comes down" or in agreement with the preceding "bread" (*artos*) as "*that* which came down."[13] In other words, the multitude may have heard "the bread of God is *that* which came down from heaven," which they took to mean the word of the Lord, or the law that came from heaven, rather than the Son of God who Himself would give life. Thus, in the first part of His teaching to the multitude Jesus had led them away from their previous expectations of who He was—He was not, in this first coming, a political deliverer and an earthly king, nor was He merely a miracle worker who could provide for His people's needs and usher in the new messianic age of peace and prosperity. By identifying Himself as the Bread of Life, He corrected the idea that He was a new prophet and giver of law in the mode of Moses.

In the section of Jesus's words to the multitude (vv. 35–40), He begins to explain why He had come into the world,

"I am the bread of life: he that cometh to me shall never hunger; and he that believeth on me shall never thirst" (v. 35). This resonates immediately with Jesus's words to the woman of Samaria in the Water of Life discourse (John 4:4–42), in which Jesus had said, "But whosoever drinketh of the water that I shall give him shall never thirst; but the water that I shall give him shall be in him a well of water springing up into everlasting life" (John 4:14).[14] Thus, Jesus combines the symbolism in Exodus of manna and the water that came from the rock (see Exodus 17:6; Deuteronomy 8:15), a fact confirmed by Paul: "Moreover, brethren, I would not that ye should be ignorant, how that all our fathers . . . did all eat the same spiritual meat; and did all drink the same spiritual drink: for they drank of that spiritual Rock that followed them: and that Rock was Christ" (1 Corinthians 10:1–4).

Here in the first part of the discourse, Jesus makes no explicit reference to eating the Bread of Life, saying simply that those who come to Him will not hunger. The earlier images of eating manna and eating the word of the Lord, however, made this implicit, albeit still comfortably metaphorical. Here and throughout the discourse, the symbol of eating powerfully represents accepting Jesus fully and internalizing Him and what He represents. A precedent for this may be found in the Bread of the Presence (*lechem panim*, KJV "shewbread") used in the Tabernacle and both Jerusalem temples. The Bread of the Presence represented the presence of the Lord in the temple and was "most holy," meaning that it conveyed holiness to those who touched it—in this instance, to the priests who ate it each week.[15]

### "The Bread of Life Sermon"

Like the manna sent from heaven, Jesus testified, "For I came down from heaven, not to do mine own will, but the will of him that sent me" (John 6:38); this answers the Christological questions regarding the person and work of the Christ in a single pronouncement. As a proclamation on the person of Jesus, "came down from heaven" is an identification of His divine origins, a proclamation used by Jesus with Nicodemus (see John 3:13) and by John the Baptist with his disciples (John 3:31). Thus, Jesus was not simply a messiah in a general sense—an anointed Davidic king or an anointed high priest—rather He was *the* Messiah, the one who came down from heaven. As for the work of the Messiah, He did not come to do His own will but the will of the one who sent Him.

#### Words to "the Jews" (6:41–59)

Up to this point, John has described Jesus's audience as the multitude (*ho ochlos*) translated variously in the KJV as "the multitude" (v. 2), "the company" (v. 5), and "the people" (vv. 22, 24). Suddenly, in this second section of the sermon, John's description of the audience shifts to a group he calls *hoi Ioudaioi*, or "the Jews" (vv. 41, 52).[16] This shift may also signal a change of scene from the harbor or some other outdoor setting where the crowd first found Jesus to the synagogue in Capernaum, which verse 59 indicates to be the place where much of the discourse was delivered.[17] While members of the multitude and certainly many of Jesus's disciples may have followed Him into the synagogue and heard this second part of His discourse, the sudden change of tone and markedly sharper rhetoric in verses 41–59 strongly suggests that Jesus is focusing His attention on a new, more hostile audience.

The members of the multitude that Jesus has already addressed and His own followers, whom He will speak to in the final part of the discourse, were all Jewish. Clearly "the Jews" who are the target of Jesus's harsher words here are a specific group, generally regarded as the religious and political leadership who increasingly opposed Him during His ministry.[18] According to this view, "the Jews" of verses 41 and 52 include either the national leadership or the local aristocracy and religious leaders. This is in line with the observation of Elder James E. Talmage: "There were present in the synagogue some rulers—Pharisees, scribes, rabbis—and these, designated collectively as the Jews, criticized Jesus. . . . Chiefly to this class rather than to the promiscuous crowd who had hastened after him, Jesus appears to have addressed the remainder of his discourse."[19]

Like the teachings to the multitude, this part of the discourse contains two sections. The first section, the murmurs of "the Jews" and Jesus's response to them, focuses largely on the issue of who Jesus is (vv. 41–50). The second, through the jarring image of flesh and blood, concentrates on the central act of Jesus's work, His salvific death, and believers' acceptance and incorporation of it (vv. 51–59).

In the first section "the Jews" have a particular, and increasingly violent, theological reaction to who Jesus testifies that He is. Their murmuring results directly from Jesus's claim that He is "the bread that came down from

## "The Bread of Life Sermon"

heaven" (v. 41), which identifies Him as the Son of the Father. To counter this claim, they respond by charging: "Is not this Jesus, the son of Joseph, whose father and mother we know? how is it then that he saith, I came down from heaven?" (v. 43). Their emphasis on Jesus's presumed parentage suggests that they fully understood the implications of the claim that Jesus had come down from heaven. By attributing Jesus's paternity to Joseph the carpenter, the synagogue leadership is clearly trying to negate Jesus's claim to be God's Son; its murmuring echoes the murmuring of the children of Israel against both Moses and the Lord during the Exodus, which was later understood to be caused by unbelief (see Psalm 106:23–25).[20] Furthermore, disbelieving Jesus's testimony, "the Jews" are repeating the mistake of their fathers in the wilderness and keeping themselves from coming to Christ; consequently, Jesus's pointed statement "Your fathers did eat manna in the wilderness, and are dead" (6:49) takes on particular significance for this audience.

The Christological error of the multitude has mostly concerned what Jesus would do, but once they begin to grasp the idea that He has come to give new bread as Moses—or God through Moses—gave them the law, they are eager to accept "this bread." On the other hand, "the Jews," resistant to changing their idea of who Jesus was, cling more tenaciously to Moses and the old law. Although Moses is not explicitly named, the return to the theme of manna in the wilderness, which represents the Lord's sustaining His people in the wilderness and also typified Moses's giving of the law, compares the law of Moses unfavorably to the grace of Christ: "For the law was given by Moses, but grace and truth came by Jesus Christ" (John 1:17).[21] For them, manna represents both the miracles that the Lord worked for their fathers through Moses and the law that He gave through Moses. Those ancestors received the means to maintain their physical lives for a season, but they are now dead; likewise the law that the manna represents failed to give life. Jesus, on the other hand, is "the bread which cometh down from heaven, that a man may eat thereof, and not die" (v. 50).

The focus of the second section of Jesus's address to "the Jews" shifts to the central act of His role as the Christ, or Anointed One: His salvific death whereby He brought life to the world. Describing this gift as giving His flesh immediately leads the *Ioudaioi* to complain, "How can this man give us his flesh to eat?" (v. 52). This complaint seems disingenuous since even the broader crowd has understood bread as a symbol for the law, and those educated in religious discussions and imagery should have seen that Jesus was using a metaphor.[22] In response to their reaction, Jesus extends the metaphor: "Verily, verily, I say unto you, except ye eat the flesh of the Son of man, and drink his blood, ye have no life in you. Whoso eateth my flesh, and drinketh my blood, hath eternal life; and I will raise him up at the last day" (vv. 53–54). Modern, particularly Christian, readers—accustomed to the sacramental imagery of partaking of bread and either wine or water which represents the body and blood of Christ—may not always appreciate the impact of this imagery on its original audience. Given biblical injunctions against consuming blood,[23] the addition of "drinketh my blood"

## "The Bread of Life Sermon"

sharpened the rejection from "the Jews," but this is vital for correctly understanding Jesus's teaching here.

The Exodus imagery of the discourse's Passover setting provides an important, although often overlooked, image that connects this flesh and blood symbolism directly to the original discourse that Jesus delivered—namely, the Paschal Lamb which was sacrificed so that its blood would ward off death and whose flesh was eaten in a festive meal. Nevertheless, comparisons between the sacrament of the Lord's Supper and the flesh and blood section of the Bread of Life discourse must be qualified, however, because the symbolism of the sacrament is actually much broader than Jesus's statement here. While the sacrament is certainly commemorative, causing Christians since Jesus's mortal ministry to look back at both His suffering and His death, the fact that it is to be celebrated specifically until He comes again (see 1 Corinthians 11:26; Matthew 26:29; Mark 14:25; Luke 22:18) suggests that it can also, in a sense, be proleptic—anticipating His glorious return and foreshadowing the great end-time messianic feast (see Isaiah 25:6–8; Ezekiel 39:17–20; Zechariah 9:15; D&C 27:4–14).

Perhaps this is why all sacramental references in the New Testament are to the body (*sōma*: Matthew 26:26; Mark 14:22; Luke 22:19; 1 Corinthians 11:24, 27, 29) of Jesus rather than specifically to the flesh (*sarx/sarka*: John 6:51, 53–55).[24] Jesus's institution of the sacrament among the Nephites may illustrate the difference, since to them He explains that the sacramental bread is "in remembrance of my body, *which I have shown to you*" (3 Nephi 18:7; emphasis added), referring in that instance to

His resurrected, immortal body as opposed to the mortal body of His earthly ministry. As both a commemorative and a proleptic act, the celebration of the sacrament in Latter-day Saint theology therefore not only looks back to His atoning death, but also looks forward to the Resurrection—emphasizing the possibility of current and future communion with Him.[25]

Although this distinction between body (*sōma*) and flesh (*sarx*) should not be pressed too far,[26] the combination of flesh and blood suggests that Jesus was speaking of His mortal body because the phrase "flesh and blood" consistently refers to living, albeit mortal, bodies (see Ether 3:8–9; Leviticus 17:11–14; Ecclesiastes 14:19; 1 Corinthians 15:50), as contrasted with "flesh and bone," which can refer to immortal, resurrected bodies (see D&C 129:1–2; 130:22).[27] Therefore, while Jesus's blood was shed both in Gethsemane and on Calvary (see Luke 22:44; Mosiah 3:7; D&C 19:16–19),[28] the Bread of Life discourse seems to focus on His Crucifixion. Thus, the sacrament is a memorial of a wider range of Jesus's atoning acts—His suffering, death, resurrection, and return in glory to live with His Saints—while the flesh and blood in the final section of the Bread of Life discourse refer more narrowly to the fact that Jesus has really come in the flesh and that He, the Lamb of God, did so to sacrifice that flesh for His people.

While the imagery of the sacrament overlaps in many ways with the imagery of the Bread of Life sermon, interpreting the discourse backwards with the ordinance that Jesus established at the end of His mortal ministry can limit our current understanding of both. The sacrament

"The Bread of Life Sermon"

holds a wider range of symbolism—especially for the body (*sōma*)—but the flesh and blood in the last portion of the Bread of Life sermon illustrate a particular Christological point about the work of Jesus, specifically the salvific nature of His death: eternal life is found only in Jesus as the Son of God who came down from heaven to die for the world, a fact that "the Jews" placing their trust in Moses and the law, could not accept.

## WORDS TO THE DISCIPLES AND TWELVE (6:60–71)

At the conclusion of the Bread of Life sermon, Jesus moves out of the synagogue and addresses the final groups mentioned in John 6: "the disciples" (vv. 60, 66) and "the Twelve" (vv. 67, 71).[29] Whereas the crowd created an incorrect idea about Jesus's person and work and "the Jews" rejected the truth when He taught it to them, Jesus's followers, collectively referred to as "his disciples" (v. 61), do not reject the idea of a divine Son who came down from heaven: they accept who Jesus is. Indeed the Twelve had a particular testimony of this. Nevertheless, many of the disciples do not understand or cannot accept what Jesus has come to do as it is represented by "flesh and blood" passages of the sermon—namely that He has come to die for His people. While these passages are disturbing if taken literally, even for those disciples who may understand that the passages are a metaphor for accepting the death of Jesus, they prove to be "a hard saying." The disciples also begin to murmur at the proposal that their Messiah will need to give His flesh and blood by dying.

The general reaction of the disciples here parallels the reaction of the Twelve to Jesus when He began to teach them more directly that He must go to Jerusalem to suffer and die, as told in the synoptics. In the three great predictions of His coming suffering, Peter and the other Apostles, who have gained a great testimony by revelation of who Jesus is, still find it hard to embrace what He must do.[30] Elder McConkie wrote: "By the simple expedient of teaching strong doctrine to the hosts that followed him, Jesus was able to separate the chaff from the wheat and choose out those who were worthy of membership in his earthly kingdom. Before entering the synagogue in Capernaum to preach his great discourse on the Bread of Life, Jesus was at the height of his popularity . . . [but] unable to believe and accept his strong and plain assertions about eating his flesh and drinking his blood, even many classified as disciples fell away."[31]

John records that "from that time many of his disciples went back, and walked no more with him," at which point Jesus, turning to His final audience, poignantly asks the Twelve, "Will ye also go away?" (6:6–67). Peter's response, "Lord, to whom shall we go? Thou hast the words of eternal life. And we believe and are sure that thou art that Christ, the Son of the living God" (6:68–69),[32] contrasts sharply with the position of "the Jews" in the discourse on the Divine Son (5:39): Jesus, not the Jewish scriptures, has the words of eternal life. Peter and the other Apostles now understand the answer to the first part of the Christological question, who Jesus is. While they may not yet fully understand why He must die, their determination to follow Him after the Bread of Life discourse reflects their growing faith in Him. Doubtlessly the complete meaning of Jesus's "flesh and

## "The Bread of Life Sermon"

blood," which focuses the "work" of Jesus on the necessity of His giving His life for the life of the world, is not clear to the Twelve or to any of the disciples until after the Passion and Resurrection. Then, however, it would become the central focus of the apostolic proclamation.

That the Son of God came down from heaven and became flesh and that He laid that flesh down and shed His blood is the fundamental definition of the gospel that believers must accept and internalize. What Jesus taught in metaphor in the Bread of Life discourse He taught directly to the Nephites after His Resurrection:

> And my Father sent me that I might be lifted up upon the cross; and after that I had been lifted up upon the cross, that I might draw all men unto me, that as I have been lifted up by men even so should men be lifted up by the Father, to stand before me, to be judged of their works, whether they be good or whether they be evil—
>
> And for this cause have I been lifted up; therefore, according to the power of the Father I will draw all men unto me, that they may be judged according to their works.
>
> And it shall come to pass, that whoso repenteth and is baptized in my name shall be filled; and if he endureth to the end, behold, him will I hold guiltless before my Father at that day when I shall stand to judge the world. (3 Nephi 27:14–16)

Elder McConkie taught that for the Latter-day Saints and all Christians today, "to eat the flesh and drink the blood of the Son of God is, first, to accept him in the most literal and full sense, with no reservation whatever, as the personal offspring in the flesh of the Eternal Father," and working the works of God is, in practical terms, "keep[ing] the commandments of the Son by accepting his gospel, joining his Church, and enduring in obedience and righteousness unto the end."[33] To this we can add a lesson from "the Jews" and those early disciples who could not easily accept that their Messiah had come to die: part of accepting Jesus as the Son of God includes accepting—indeed focusing on—the salvific necessity of His suffering, death, and Resurrection that constitutes the true meaning of Easter.

NOTES

1. The seven discourses in John are the New Birth (3:1–36), the Water of Life (4:1–42), the Divine Son (5:17–47), the Bread of Life (6:35–58), the Life-Giving Spirit (7:16–52), the Light of the World (8:12–59), and the Good Shepherd (10:1–18).

2. See the surveys of scholarship by Vernon Ruland, "Sign and Sacrament: John's Bread of Life Discourse," in *Interpretation, a Journal of Bible and Theology* 18 (1964): 450–52; Leon Morris, *The Gospel According to John*, rev. ed., The New International Greek Commentary on the New Testament (Grand Rapids, MI: Eerdmans, 1995), 313–15; and Raymond E. Brown, *An Introduction to the Gospel of John*, Francis J. Moloney, ed. (New York: Doubleday, 2003), 229–233. G. H. C. MacGregor, "The Eucharist in the Fourth Gospel," in *New Testament Studies* 9 (1962–63): 114, observes that confessional biases have tended to

"THE BREAD OF LIFE SERMON"

affect the interpretation of the discourse, Catholic writers generally interpreting it sacramentally and conservative Protestants denying any reference to the sacrament.

3. Bruce R. McConkie, *Doctrinal New Testament Commentary* (Salt Lake City: Bookcraft, 1988), 358.
4. John Painter, *The Quest for the Messiah: The History, Literature, and Theology of the Johannine Community*, 2nd ed. (Edinburgh: T&T Clark, 1993), 264. For an older, yet detailed, discussion, see Bertil Gärtner, "John 6 and the Jewish Passover," *Coniectanea Neotestamentica* 17 (Copenhagen: Ejnar Munksgaard, 1959), 14–19.
5. John M. Perry, "The Sacramental Tradition in the Fourth Gospel and the Synoptics," in *Jesus in the Johannine Tradition*, Robert T. Fortna and Tom Thatcher, ed. (Louisville: Westminster John Knox, 1989), 157, calls this "a eucharistic midrash on the Exodus story." See also C. H. Dodd, *The Interpretation of the Fourth Gospel* (Cambridge: Cambridge University Press, 1958), 335.
6. Simply translated, *egō eimi* means "I am," and when used by Jesus, the formula sometimes appears as a simple self-identification (John 6:20, "*I* that speak unto thee *am he*"), with a predicate (for instance, John 9:5, "*I am* the light of the world"), or absolutely without a predicate (John 8:58, "Verily, verily, I say unto you, Before Abraham was, *I am*"). See the detailed discussion of Brown, *An Introduction to the Gospel of John*, 533–38, and Catrin H. Williams, "'I Am' or 'I Am He'?" in *Jesus in the Johannine Tradition*, Robert T. Fortna and Tom Thatcher, ed. (Louisville: Westminster John Knox, 2001), 343–48.
7. As in the earlier stilling of the storm recorded by the synoptics (Matthew 8:18–27; Mark 4:35–41; Luke 8:22–25),

the raging sea resonates with the image found in both the Old Testament and throughout Near Eastern mythology of the great deep representing the surging force of uncreated chaos. See Williams, "'I Am' or 'I Am He'?" 346.

8. Bertil Gärtner, "John 6 and the Jewish Passover," 18; see also Brown, *An Introduction to the Gospel of John*, 245; Valletta, "John's Testimony of the Bread of Life," 182.
9. See Brown, *An Introduction to the Gospel of John*, 1:265.
10. 2 Baruch 29:8.
11. Morris, *The Gospel According to John*, 301.
12. Dodd, *The Interpretation of the Fourth Gospel*, 336–37; Gärtner, "John 6 and the Jewish Passover," 41; Morris, *The Gospel According to John*, 319.
13. Brown, *An Introduction to the Gospel of John*, 262–63; Painter, *The Quest for the Messiah*, 273; Morris, *The Gospel According to John*, 322–23.
14. Painter, *The Quest for the Messiah*, 269–70. After the dialogue with the Samaritan woman, Jesus told His disciples, "I have meat [*brōsin*, or "food"] to eat that ye know not of" (John 4:32), a foreshadowing perhaps of this very discourse.
15. Margaret Barker, *The Great High Priest: The Temple Roots of Christian Liturgy* (New York: T&T Clark, 2003), 70, 87–91, 93, 274.
16. Painter, *Quest for the Messiah*, 267.
17. Painter, *Quest for the Messiah*, 253, 278; Morris, *The Gospel According to John*, 327. Talmage, *Jesus the Christ* (Salt Lake City: Deseret Book, 1984), 339, however, places the entire discourse in the synagogue, and Gärtner, "John 6 and the Jewish Passover," 14–19, makes an interesting argument that connects explicitly the feeding, walking on

water, and Bread of Life sermon with the Jewish texts that may have been read in the Capernaum synagogue as part of a Passover festival for those who could not travel to Jerusalem for the feast.

18. John's use of *hoi Ioudaioi* throughout his gospel is problematic and has been the focus of much debate in studies of John's writings. For a detailed discussion of the meaning of "the Jews" in John, see Eric Huntsman, "The Bread of Life Sermon," in *The Life and Teachings of Jesus Christ: From the Transfiguration through the Triumphal Entry*, ed. Richard Neitzel Holzapfel and Thomas A. Wayment (Salt Lake City: Deseret Book, 2006), 273–75.
19. Talmage, *Jesus the Christ*, 341.
20. Painter, *Quest for the Messiah*, 279; Morris, *The Gospel According to John*, 327n111.
21. Dodd, *The Interpretation of the Fourth Gospel*, 337.
22. Talmage, *Jesus the Christ*, 342, 347–47n10.
23. Note that the Old Testament injunctions against drinking blood (see Genesis 9:4; Leviticus 19:26) were reaffirmed in the New Testament (see Acts 15:30; 21:25).
24. See Morris, *The Gospel According to John*, 331–32, especially note 125. For the semantic ranges of the respective nouns, see Frederick William Danker, ed., *A Greek-English Lexicon of the New Testament and Other Early Christian Literature*, 3rd ed. (Chicago: University of Chicago Press, 2000), "sarx" and "sōma," 743–44, 799–800.
25. Bruce R. McConkie, *Doctrinal New Testament Commentary* (Salt Lake City: Deseret Book, 1965–73), 1:724. McConkie further states, "Jesus promises, at his Second Coming, to again partake of the sacrament with the Twelve, or rather the eleven, for without doubt Judas

had already fled into the darkness of the night. This same promise was expanded by modern revelation to include Joseph Smith and the worthy modern-day Saints, as also Moroni, Elias, John the Baptist, Elijah, Abraham, Isaac, Jacob, Joseph who was sold into Egypt, Adam, and by necessary implication the righteous of all ages (Doctrine and Covenants 27:1–12)."

26. Third Nephi 18:28–29, for instance, speaks of partaking of the sacrament improperly as "partaking of my flesh and blood unworthily," although this may have particular reference to improperly trying to lay hold of the fruits of the Atonement, being somewhat analogous to "crucifying the Lord afresh" (Hebrews 6:6) and even "assenting unto his death" (D&C 132:27). On the other hand, see also Doctrine and Covenants 20:40, which refers to "administering the bread and wine—the emblems of the flesh and blood."

27. "After the resurrection from the dead our bodies will be spiritual bodies, but they will be bodies that are tangible, bodies that have been purified, but they will nevertheless be bodies of flesh and bones, but they will not be blood bodies, they will no longer be quickened by blood but quickened by the spirit which is eternal and they shall become immortal and shall never die" (Joseph Fielding Smith, in Conference Report, April 1917, 63).

28. See Andrew C. Skinner, *Gethsemane* (Salt Lake City: Deseret Book, 2002), 76–78.

29. Painter, *Quest for the Messiah*, 267.

30. First prediction: Matthew 16:21–23; Mark 8:31–9:1; Luke 9:19–27. Second prediction: Matthew 17:22–23; Mark

"THE BREAD OF LIFE SERMON"

9:30–37; Luke 9:43b–45. Third prediction: Matthew 20:17–19; Mark 10:32–45; Luke 18:31–34.
31. McConkie, *Doctrinal New Testament Commentary*, 1:361.
32. Although harmonizing events in John with the synoptics is difficult, Peter's confession following the Bread of Life discourse appears to anticipate that which he delivers at Caesarea Philippi shortly before the Transfiguration (see Matthew 16:13–20; Mark 8:27–30; Luke 9:19–21; see Ruland, "Sign and Sacrament," 452).
33. McConkie, *Doctrinal New Testament Commentary*, 1:358.

FRANK F. JUDD JR.

# JESUS CHRIST: THE SAVIOR WHO KNOWS

Jesus knows and loves us. This is a powerful and reassuring reality of the restored gospel. The resurrected Savior declared this truth to the Nephites: "I know my sheep, and they are numbered" (3 Nephi 18:31; see also John 10:14, 27). But what does it mean that Jesus knows us? This truth extends beyond the Savior's knowledge of our identity. Elder Richard G. Scott taught, "The Savior knows you; he loves you and is aware of your specific needs."[1] Our Redeemer does not have just a superficial knowledge, but rather He personally understands our true identity, our innermost needs, and our eternal potential. This chapter explores what Jesus Christ knows about each one of us, how He gained that intimate knowledge, and most importantly, why it is imperative that we are aware of this glorious

---

Frank F. Judd Jr. is an assistant professor of ancient scripture at Brigham Young University.

truth. I hope that a clearer understanding of these issues will foster a deeper comprehension of the life, death, and Resurrection of our Savior, and result in a greater and more joyful appreciation of the Easter celebration.

## DIFFERENT KINDS OF KNOWLEDGE

Two essential ways of gaining knowledge are by study and by experience.[2] Both means are important. The Lord commanded the Prophet Joseph Smith to learn through his own research: "Study and learn, and become acquainted with all good books, and with languages, tongues, and people" (D&C 90:15; see also 88:118; 109:7, 14). Joseph Smith was also informed concerning his suffering in Liberty Jail, "All these things shall give thee experience, and shall be for thy good" (D&C 122:7).

Some languages, such as the Greek of the New Testament, contain different words to distinguish these kinds of knowledge. While they overlap slightly in meaning, the Greek verb *oida* means "to have information about," while the verb *ginōskō* can refer to "familiarity acquired through experience or association with a pers[on] or thing."[3] Unfortunately, however, in the King James Version of the New Testament both of these separate and distinct Greek words are translated into English as the verb "to know." For instance, the Savior taught that we should know the information contained in the scriptures. In the Gospel of Matthew when Jesus rebuked a group of Sadducees, the Greek word for knowledge of facts is used: "Ye do err, not knowing [*oida*] the scriptures" (Matthew 22:29). On the other hand, Jesus also emphasized the need for knowledge

## "Jesus Christ: The Savior Who Knows"

by experience. In the Savior's famous Intercessory Prayer, the Gospel of John uses the Greek word for experiential knowledge: "And this is life eternal, that they might know [*ginōskō*] thee the only true God, and Jesus Christ, whom thou hast sent" (John 17:3). This example underscores how deeply we must come to know God the Father and His Son Jesus Christ to gain eternal life.[4]

Modern revelation reinforces the link between gaining knowledge and gaining salvation: "It is impossible for a man to be saved in ignorance" (D&C 131:6). Certainly, studying the scriptures and other good literature helps us build an essential foundation. But scriptural or literary knowledge is not the ultimate requirement for salvation. The Prophet Joseph Smith clarified: "Reading the experience of others, or the revelation given to *them*, can never give *us* a comprehensive view of our condition and true relation to God. *Knowledge of these things can only be obtained by experience* through the ordinances of God set forth for that purpose. Could you gaze into heaven five minutes, you would know more than you would by reading all that ever was written on the subject."[5] In addition to learning through participation in sacred ordinances and receiving revelation, experiential knowledge can also be gained by internalizing gospel principles. President David O. McKay taught:

> Gaining knowledge is one thing and applying it, quite another. Wisdom is the right application of knowledge; and true education—the education for which the Church stands—is the application of knowledge to the development of a noble and Godlike

character. A man may possess a profound knowledge of history and of mathematics; he may be [an] authority in psychology, biology, or astronomy; he may know all the discovered truths pertaining to geology and natural science; but if he has not with his knowledge the nobility of soul which prompts him to deal justly with his fellow men, to practise virtue and holiness in personal life, he is not a truly educated man. Character is the true aim of education.[6]

How does a wise person come to "know the only true God and Jesus Christ" by experience in the way the Savior intended? John the Beloved gave the answer: "And hereby we do know that we know him, *if we keep his commandments*. He that saith, I know him, and keepeth not his commandments, is a liar" (1 John 2:3–4; emphasis added).[7] The most important knowledge is gained by experience—specifically through revelation and obedience to the commandments of God. Thus, the Lord has explained, "Whatever principle of intelligence we attain unto in this life, it will rise with us in the resurrection. And if a person gains more knowledge and intelligence in this life *through his diligence and obedience* than another, he will have so much the advantage in the world to come" (D&C 130:18–19; emphasis added).[8]

Certain knowledge can be acquired only by those who are obedient. President Gordon B. Hinckley has taught: "Those who live the Word of Wisdom know the truth of the Word of Wisdom. Those who engage in missionary service know the divine wisdom behind that service. Those who are making an effort to strengthen their families in

"Jesus Christ: The Savior Who Knows"

obedience to the call of the Lord know that they reap the blessings of doing so. Those who engage in temple work know the truth of that work, its divine and eternal implications. Those who pay their tithing know the divine promise underlying that great law, the law of finance for the Church. Those who keep the Sabbath know the divine wisdom which provided for the Sabbath day. . . . Simply live the gospel, and everyone who does so will receive in his heart a conviction of the truth of that which he lives."[9] These principles of gaining knowledge through experience and obedience also apply to Jesus Christ.

## THE SAVIOR'S PERSONAL KNOWLEDGE

Our Savior is omniscient, all-knowing in both senses of the word *knowledge*—by study and by experience. The prophet Jacob taught: "O the greatness of the mercy of our God, the Holy One of Israel. . . . For he knoweth all things, and there is not anything save he knows it" (2 Nephi 9:19–20).[10] Further, in a modern revelation the Savior declared that He is "the same which knoweth all things, for all things are present before mine eyes" (D&C 38:2; see also John 16:30).[11]

The Joseph Smith Translation emphasizes the fact that during His lifetime, Jesus did not depend upon earthly teachers to the same degree that others did: "Jesus grew up with his brethren, and waxed strong, and waited upon the Lord for the time of his ministry to come. And he served under his father, and he spake not as other men, neither could he be taught; for he needed not that any man should teach him" (Joseph Smith Translation, Matthew 3:23).[12]

Despite His divine Sonship, Jesus also gained knowledge as a mortal being, line upon line and precept upon precept. While growing up in Nazareth, "Jesus increased in wisdom and stature, and in favor with God and man" (Luke 2:52).[13]

Jesus gained factual knowledge by study, especially study of the scriptures. He knew the Old Testament scriptures thoroughly and often cited passages during His sermons (see Matthew 5:21–47). While fasting in the wilderness of Judea, the Savior quoted specific scriptures in order to counter Satan's temptations (see Matthew 4:1–11; Luke 4:1–13).[14] At a synagogue in Nazareth, Jesus read from the scriptures and proclaimed Himself to be the fulfillment of prophecy (see Luke 4:16–21). On the road to Emmaus, the resurrected Savior walked with some disciples and "beginning at Moses and all the prophets, he expounded unto them in all the scriptures the things concerning himself" (Luke 24:27). As Jehovah, the premortal Savior said, "I am more intelligent than they all" (Abraham 3:19).[15] Concerning this, Elder Neal A. Maxwell explained: "This means that Jesus knows more about astrophysics than all the humans who have ever lived, who live now, and who will yet live. Likewise, the same may be said about any other topic or subject. Moreover, what the Lord knows is, fortunately, *vastly* more—not just *barely* more—than the combination of what all mortals know."[16]

The Savior also gained knowledge by His own experience during His earthly sojourn, encountering the same types of situations that all mortals do. King Benjamin prophesied that Jesus would "suffer temptations, and pain of body, hunger, thirst, and fatigue" (Mosiah 3:7).[17]

## "Jesus Christ: The Savior Who Knows"

During His mortal ministry, Jesus also knew that He was going to suffer and die for the sins of the world (see Matthew 16:21; 17:22–23; 28:18–19). The Savior's own experience through obedience to His Father, however, perfected that knowledge. As Elder Maxwell has explained: "Jesus knew cognitively what He must do, but not experientially. He had never personally known the exquisite and exacting process of an atonement before. Thus, when the agony came in its fulness, it was so much, much worse than even He with his unique intellect had ever imagined!"[18]

### THE SAVIOR'S VICARIOUS KNOWLEDGE OF SIN

Another dimension of the Savior's knowledge is the fact that He knows what we go through when we sin. As stated above, Jesus understands us because His mortal life, full of temptations, was similar to that of all human beings. A key difference, however, distinguishes the Savior's mortal experience from ours. As the Apostle Paul taught concerning us, "All have sinned, and come short of the glory of God" (Romans 3:23). But Jesus Christ "was in all points tempted like as we are, *yet without sin*" (Hebrews 4:15; emphasis added).[19] How can our Savior really understand what it is like to give in to temptation, when He never committed a sin? The answer lies in the Savior's experience of the Atonement.[20]

Because of His mortal life, Jesus knows what it is like to be tempted, but because of His experience in the Garden of Gethsemane and on the cross,[21] Jesus vicariously knows our experience with sin. The resurrected Savior declared to the Nephites concerning His experience, "I have drunk out of that bitter cup which the Father hath given me, and have glorified the Father in *taking upon me the sins of the world*, in the which I have suffered the will of the Father in all things from the beginning" (3 Nephi 11:11; emphasis added).[22] While the Savior prayed in the Garden of Gethsemane following the Last Supper, He was in such agony that "his sweat was as it were great drops of blood falling down to the ground" (Luke 22:44).[23] What made Jesus sweat blood from His pores?

It was, of course, the incomprehensible experience of taking upon Himself the sins of the world. There is symbolic meaning in the name of the place where these things occurred. Significantly, the Hebrew name *Gethsemane* means "oil press."[24] Elder Russell M. Nelson explained that in the place where Jesus suffered, "olives had been pressed under the weight of great stone wheels to squeeze precious oil from the olives. So the Christ in the Garden of Gethsemane was literally pressed under the weight of the sins of the world. He sweated great drops of blood— his life's 'oil'—which issued from every pore."[25] But there seems to be a specific element that directly contributed to this horrible physical reaction.

While upon the cross Jesus cried out, "My God, my God, why hast thou forsaken me?" (Matthew 27:46). It may be hard for some to imagine that God would really forsake, or leave behind, His Only Begotten Son. But that is exactly what happened. President Brigham Young taught: "At the very moment, at the hour when the crisis came for him to offer up his life, *the Father withdrew Himself, withdrew His Spirit*, and cast a vail [sic] over him. That is what made him

## "Jesus Christ: The Savior Who Knows"

sweat blood. If he had had the power of God upon him, he would not have sweat blood; but all was withdrawn from him, and a veil was cast over him, and he then pled with the Father not to forsake him."[26] It is true that in Gethsemane "there appeared an angel unto him [Christ] from heaven, strengthening him" (Luke 22:43). But this support seems to have been temporary, for according to the Savior's own allusion to the presses of Gethsemane, He declared: "I have trodden the wine-press alone . . . and none were with me" (D&C 133:50; see also 76:107; 88:106; Isaiah 63:3).

According to President Young, the withdrawal of the Spirit seems to be the key to understanding why the Savior sweat blood in the Garden of Gethsemane. The Spirit (and a supporting angel) had been providing Jesus with protection from the full extent of His vicarious suffering. The Lord once taught Martin Harris concerning His experience in the garden:

> I, God, have suffered these things for all, that they might not suffer if they would repent;
>
> But if they would not repent they must suffer even as I;
>
> Which suffering caused myself, even God, the greatest of all, to tremble because of pain, and to bleed at every pore. . . .
>
> Wherefore, I command you again to repent, lest I humble you with my almighty power; and that you confess your sins, lest you suffer these punishments of which I have spoken, *of which in the smallest, yea, even in the least degree you have tasted at the time I withdrew my Spirit.* (D&C 19:16–20; emphasis added)[27]

This revelation reaffirms that unrepented sin and the loss of the Spirit cause terrible suffering. It also confirms that when Martin Harris sinned and lost the Spirit, he experienced the same kind of suffering, though a miniscule portion that the Savior experienced in Gethsemane when He bled from every pore.[28] Conversely, this scripture shows that in the Garden of Gethsemane, Jesus Christ experienced what humans experience when they sin—suffering as a result of the loss of the Spirit of the Lord.[29] Because of the withdrawal of the Spirit, the Savior suffered for the sins of the world *to the fullest degree* and sweat blood from His pores.[30]

Why would God the Father withdraw His Spirit from His Beloved Son in His hour of need? As with Martin Harris, the Holy Ghost withdraws from us when we sin. The Lord has declared in the latter days, "He that repents not, from him shall be taken even the light which he has received; for my Spirit shall not always strive with man" (D&C 1:33; see also Genesis 6:3; 1 Nephi 7:14; 2 Nephi 26:11; Ether 2:15; Moses 8:17). When Jesus took upon Himself the sins of the world, He vicariously—but literally—became guilty in our behalf. The Apostle Paul taught, "Christ hath redeemed us from the curse of the law, *being made a curse for us*" (Galatians 3:13; emphasis added).[31] In another epistle, Paul further taught that God "made him [Christ] to be sin for us" (2 Corinthians 5:21).[32] Somehow Jesus took upon Himself the sins of all mankind in a very real way—becoming "a curse" and "sin" in the process, and as a result the Father withdrew His Spirit from the Savior.[33]

Stephen E. Robinson summarized this principle: "Christ had become guilty of the sins of the world, guilty in our

## "Jesus Christ: The Savior Who Knows"

place. . . . In Gethsemane the best among us vicariously became the worst among us and suffered the very depths of hell. And as one who was guilty, the Savior experienced for the first time in his life the loss of the Spirit of God and of communion with his Father."[34] Because Jesus Christ literally took upon Himself the sins of the world, vicariously became full of sin, lost the Spirit, and experienced incomprehensible suffering, He not only knows what it is like to be tempted, but He also intimately knows what we feel like when we disobey. As a result of bearing the heavy burden of guilt and regret caused by sin, the Savior has perfect empathy for the sinful soul.

### ADDITIONAL SUFFERING AND KNOWLEDGE

The Savior's knowledge of us, however, includes much more than His comprehension of temptation and sin. How much more? The author of the Epistle to the Hebrews taught concerning Christ, "*In all things* it behoved him to be made like unto his brethren" (Hebrews 2:17; emphasis added).[35] Alma the Younger prophesied that Christ would not only experience His own "pains and afflictions and temptations of every kind" (Alma 7:11) and "take upon him[self] the sins of his people" (v. 13) but also take upon Himself the "pains," "sicknesses," and "infirmities" of mankind (vv. 11–12). According to Alma, then, in Gethsemane the Savior gained a complete comprehension not only of sin but also of other negative experiences that we go through. Elder Jeffrey R. Holland concluded that this additional suffering allowed the Savior to "bear every mortal infirmity; feel every personal heartache, sorrow, and loss."[36] Thus, because of Gethsemane, Jesus Christ not only came to fully know what we go through when we sin but also what we go through when we experience grief and sorrow that has nothing to do with sinful behavior.[37]

Why did Jesus undergo additional suffering—in particular those things that had nothing to do with sin? When Alma prophesied that Jesus would take upon himself the pains, sicknesses, and infirmities of mankind, he also explained that the Savior would do this "that his bowels may be filled with mercy, according to the flesh, that he may know according to the flesh how to succor his people according to their infirmities" (Alma 7:12).[38] Elder Maxwell explained from these passages that Jesus suffered in this additional way "in order that He might be filled with perfect, personal mercy and empathy and thereby know how to succor us in our infirmities. *He thus fully comprehends human suffering.*"[39] Jesus Christ really does know what it is like to be each one of us when we experience heartache and sorrow. As a result, He has full compassion for us in our individual situations.

In this way, Jesus has become the ideal judge of our eternal destiny. Only a judge who understands completely the experiences of the defendant can determine the correct verdict beyond question. Otherwise there would always be the possibility that the judge did not know some important fact that might bring about a different verdict. Concerning this, Elder Glenn L. Pace concluded: "Part of the reason the Savior suffered in Gethsemane was so that he would have an infinite compassion for us as we experience our trials

## "Jesus Christ: The Savior Who Knows"

and tribulations. Through his suffering in Gethsemane, the Savior became qualified to be the perfect judge. Not one of us will be able to approach him on the Judgment Day and say, 'You don't know what it was like.' He knows the nature of our trials better than we do, for he 'descended below them all.'"[40]

Additional scriptures shed light on the extent of our Savior's knowledge of us. Christ's knowledge of us is not merely collective; it is individual. While prophesying of the future Messiah, the prophet Isaiah declared, "When thou shalt make his soul an offering for sin, he shall see his seed" (Isaiah 53:10; see also Mosiah 14:10). After the prophet Abinadi quoted this passage to the people of King Noah, he defined those who are the "seed" of Christ: "Whosoever has heard the words of the prophets, yea, all the holy prophets who have prophesied concerning the coming of the Lord—I say unto you, that all those who have hearkened unto their words, and believed that the Lord would redeem his people, and have looked forward to that day for a remission of their sins, I say unto you, that these are his seed" (Mosiah 15:11).[41] Thus, Christ's "seed" are those who have believed the Savior and utilized His Atonement.

What did Isaiah mean that Christ would "see his seed" when He would "make his soul an offering for sin" in Gethsemane?[42] Elder Merrill J. Bateman interpreted this passage in the following way: "In the garden and on the cross, *Jesus saw each of us*," and therefore "the Savior's atonement in the garden and on the cross is intimate as well as infinite. Infinite in that it spans the eternities. Intimate in that *the Savior felt each person's pains, sufferings, and sicknesses.*"⁴³

As a result of His experience in Gethsemane, our Savior not only understands what it is like to be tempted and to give in to sin, He also has a personal knowledge of the mortal experience for each person individually. As Elder Maxwell taught, "There is no personal problem through which anyone has passed or will pass but what Jesus understands profoundly, perfectly, and personally."⁴⁴ He knows what it is like to be each one of us when we are sick, lonely, depressed, or mistreated.⁴⁵ Jesus Christ is in the ideal position to have compassion upon us, precisely because He knows us perfectly and personally, even better than we know ourselves. He therefore has become not only our perfect judge but also our perfect advocate—our perfect friend.

## PERSONAL APPLICATION

Once we understand that our Savior has a perfect knowledge of us, what should we do about it? The author of the Epistle to the Hebrews declared: "For we have not an high priest which cannot be touched with the feelings of our infirmities; but was in all points tempted like as we are, yet without sin. *Let us therefore come boldly unto the throne of grace, that we may obtain mercy, and find grace to help in time of need*" (Hebrews 4:15–16; emphasis added). The phrase "throne of grace" refers to the "mercy seat" on the top of the ark of the covenant that was placed in the Holy of Holies in the temple at Jerusalem (see Exodus 25:18–22).

## "Jesus Christ: The Savior Who Knows"

The mercy seat itself symbolized the presence of God (see Exodus 30:6). Once a year on the Day of Atonement, the high priest would enter the Holy of Holies and sprinkle the mercy seat with blood, "symbolizing the power of the Atonement to cleanse all of repentant Israel from their sins and to render them worthy to be in the presence of the Lord."[46] Coming "boldly unto the throne of grace," then, symbolizes confidently approaching our Heavenly Father in prayer in the name of His Son, the supernal high priest, in order that we might take advantage of the mercy and forgiveness available though the Atonement (see Hebrews 3:1, 5:5, 9:11).

We should not timidly seek these blessings, thinking that our Savior will not understand what we have done or what we are going through. He knows! He understands! Elder Maxwell taught, "Jesus knows and takes into account, personally and perfectly, the highly individualized situations of our 'tether and pang,' including the innermost desires and intents of our hearts."[47] Because this is so, we should confidently seek for relief through the Atonement of Jesus Christ, which includes not only forgiveness of sins, but also daily spiritual assistance to live and endure. Elder Gene R. Cook concluded: "What a glorious thought that, in truth, Jesus Christ is capable of bearing the problems and challenges that we each face in our daily lives. He will not only help us to be saved at the Judgment Day, but he and his Father will be involved with us on a regular basis if we will find access to them."[48]

Celebrating Easter

CONCLUSION

During His mortal life, Jesus learned all about temptation. In Gethsemane, Jesus learned what it is like to sin. Because of this, some may think that the Atonement relates only to repentance and forgiveness of sins. But the experience in Gethsemane also gave the Savior intimate knowledge about the mortal experience for each one of us so that He could help us. Elder Holland testified that "the Savior's Atonement lifts from us not only the burden of our sins but also the burden of our disappointments and sorrows, our heartaches and our despair" and that this knowledge gives us "a reason and a way to improve, an incentive to lay down our burdens and take up our salvation."[49]

Understanding that our Savior has a perfect knowledge of our individual condition and our unique situation, we should join hands with Him as we face the road of life ahead. The prophet Nephi declared concerning his mortal condition and relationship with the Savior: "When I desire to rejoice, my heart groaneth because of my sins; nevertheless, I know in whom I have trusted. My God hath been my support; he hath led me through mine afflictions in the wilderness" (2 Nephi 4:19–20). Jesus Christ is truly the Savior who knows. And because He knows, He is uniquely qualified both to save us from sin and to carry us through the unpredictable wilderness of our lives.

NOTES

1. Richard G. Scott, "The Power to Make a Difference," *Ensign*, November 1983, 70.

"JESUS CHRIST: THE SAVIOR WHO KNOWS"

2. For a more detailed discussion of the many ways to gain knowledge, see Gerald N. Lund, "An Anti-Christ in the Book of Mormon—The Face May Be Strange, but the Voice Is Familiar," in *Selected Writings of Gerald N. Lund* (Salt Lake City: Deseret Book, 1999), 120–22.
3. See Frederick William Danker, ed., *A Greek-English Lexicon of the New Testament and Other Early Christian Literature*, 3rd ed. (Chicago: University of Chicago Press, 2000), 693, 199.
4. It is interesting to note that this same Greek word for "knowledge by experience" is used in the Greek Old Testament (the Septuagint) to refer to the marital relationship between husband and wife (see Genesis 4:1, 17, 25). Symbolically, our covenant relationship with the Savior is often described in terms of a marriage, with Jesus as the bridegroom and Church members as the bride (see Matthew 9:14–15; 25:1–13; John 3:27–29; Revelation 19:7–9). See also Stephen E. Robinson, *Believing Christ* (Salt Lake City: Deseret Book, 1992), 24–25.
5. Joseph Smith, *Teachings of the Prophet Joseph Smith* (Salt Lake City: Deseret Book, 1976), 324; emphasis added. Note also Elder Jeffrey R. Holland's comments: "Sometimes we seek heaven too obliquely, focusing on programs or history or the experience of others. Those are important but not as important as personal experience, true discipleship, and the strength that comes from experiencing firsthand the majesty of His touch" ("Broken Things to Mend," *Ensign*, May 2006, 70).
6. David O. McKay, *Gospel Ideals* (Salt Lake City: Improvement Era, 1953), 440. Concerning this, Elder Neal A. Maxwell taught: "Knowledge—discovery, its preservation,

its perpetuation—is very important. Yet, being knowledgeable while leaving undeveloped the virtues of love, mercy, meekness, and patience is not enough for full discipleship. Mere intellectual assent to a truth deprives us of the relevant, personal experiences that come from applying what we profess to believe. There were probably orientation briefings in the premortal world about how this mortal life would unfold for us, but the real experience is another thing! Thus, while knowledge is clearly very important, standing alone it cannot save us" ("Becoming a Disciple," *Ensign*, June 1996, 13–14).

7. In this verse, each instance of the English verb "to know" is a translation of the Greek word for knowledge by experience (*ginōskō*).

8. For the connection between obedience and knowledge, see John 7:17; 8:31–32; Mosiah 4:10; Alma 26:22; D&C 89:18–19.

9. Gordon B. Hinckley, *Teachings of Gordon B. Hinckley* (Salt Lake City: Deseret Book, 1997), 403–4. President Hinckley also taught: "No force on earth can stop the Almighty from pouring down knowledge . . . if we will live in righteousness, obey the principles of the gospel, do what we ought to do as members of The Church of Jesus Christ of Latter-day Saints, and walk in obedience to the commandments of God. *We will then receive enlightenment and knowledge and understanding and faith*, and our lives will be enriched and be made more happy and more fruitful" (quoted in "News of the Church," *Ensign*, October 1995, 75; emphasis added).

10. The Book of Mormon clearly teaches that "the Holy One of Israel" is Jesus Christ (see 2 Nephi 25:29; Omni 1:26).

"Jesus Christ: The Savior Who Knows"

11. See also Marion G. Romney, "My Testimony of Jesus Christ," *Ensign*, September 1974, 5.
12. See also Thomas A. Wayment, ed., *The Complete Joseph Smith Translation of the New Testament* (Salt Lake City: Deseret Book, 2005), 5.
13. Modern revelation teaches that the Savior "received not of the fulness at the first, but received grace for grace; and he received not of the fulness at first, but continued from grace to grace, until he received a fulness. And thus he was called the Son of God, because he received not of the fulness at first" (D&C 93:12–13).
14. See also Howard W. Hunter, "The Temptations of Christ," *Ensign*, November 1976, 18.
15. For Jesus's identity as Jehovah, see 3 Nephi 15:4–5 and John 8:58–59.
16. Neal A. Maxwell, *All These Things Shall Give Thee Experience* (Salt Lake City: Deseret Book, 1979), 22.
17. Besides the famous temptations in the wilderness of Judea (see Matthew 4:1–11; Luke 4:1–13), see also Matthew 16:1; 19:3; 22:8, 35. Alma prophesied that Christ would "go forth, suffering pains and afflictions and temptations of every kind" (Alma 7:11).
18. Neal A. Maxwell, "Willing to Submit," *Ensign*, May 1985, 72–73.
19. Paul taught that Christ "knew no sin" (2 Corinthians 5:21).
20. See Robinson, *Believing Christ*, 116–25.
21. Both Elder James E. Talmage and Elder Bruce R. McConkie taught that the terrible type of suffering that the Savior endured in the Garden of Gethsemane "recurred" while He was upon the cross. See James E. Talmage, *Jesus the Christ* (Salt Lake City: The Church of Jesus Christ of

Latter-day Saints, 1915), 661; Bruce R. McConkie, *A New Witness for the Articles of Faith* (Salt Lake City: Deseret Book, 1985), xiv, 289; and Bruce R. McConkie, *The Mortal Messiah* (Salt Lake City: Deseret Book, 1979–81), 4:224.

22. See also Alma 34:8: "Christ shall come among the children of men, to take upon him the transgressions of his people, and that he shall atone for the sins of the world."

23. Both the Book of Mormon and the Doctrine and Covenants confirm that the language in this scripture is to be taken literally (see Mosiah 3:7; D&C 19:18).

24. Ulrich Luz, *Matthew 21–28* (Minneapolis: Fortress Press, 2005), 395.

25. Russell M. Nelson, "Why This Holy Land?" *Ensign*, December 1989, 17–18. See also Robinson, *Believing Christ*, 119–20.

26. Brigham Young, *Journal of Discourses*, 3:206; emphasis added. On this issue, see also Robert L. Millet, "Treading the Winepress Alone," in *Studies in Scripture, Vol. 5: The Gospels* (Salt Lake City: Deseret Book, 1986), 434–35.

27. At this point in Church history, Martin Harris was having second thoughts about mortgaging part of his farm to pay for the publication of the Book of Mormon (see Stephen E. Robinson and H. Dean Garrett, *A Commentary on the Doctrine and Covenants* [Salt Lake City: Deseret Book, 2000–2005], 1:110–11).

28. Concerning these verses, Robinson and Garrett conclude: "The unrepentant will, however, each suffer *for their own sins* as [Jesus] suffered *for the sins of the world*, suffering exactly the same kind of anguish, but not to the same degree" (Robinson and Garrett, *Commentary on the Doctrine and Covenants*, 1:118; emphasis in original).

## "Jesus Christ: The Savior Who Knows"

29. Robert J. Matthews taught, "[Christ] died a physical death on the cross, and he died a 'spiritual death' in the Garden of Gethsemane (as well as on the cross) when he took upon himself the sins of all mankind" (*A Bible! A Bible!* [Salt Lake City: Bookcraft, 1990], 260).
30. The Lord has declared in modern revelation that the Savior "descended below" everything that any mortal has experienced. See D&C 122:8; 88:6. On this issue, see also Millet, "Treading the Winepress Alone," 436–38.
31. Paul was alluding to the reference in the law of Moses, where the Lord declared to ancient Israel: "If a man have committed a sin worthy of death. . . . Thou [shalt] hang him on a tree . . . for he that is hanged is accursed of God" (Deuteronomy 21:22–23).
32. Note the interpretation of C. K. Barrett: "Christ became *sin*; that is, he came to stand in that relation with God which normally is the result of sin, estranged from God and the object of his wrath" (*The Second Epistle to the Corinthians* [London: A & C Black, 1973], 180). F. F. Bruce refers to this passage from C. K. Barrett when interpreting Galatians 3:13; see *The Epistle to the Galatians* (Grand Rapids: Eerdmans, 1982), 166. In light of Barrett's interpretation of Paul that Christ became sin and the object of God's wrath, note that modern revelation calls Christ's experience in Gethsemane "the wine-press of the fierceness of the wrath of Almighty God" (D&C 76:107; see also 88:106).
33. Robert L. Millet interpreted Galatians 3:13 and 2 Corinthians 5:21 to mean the innocent man Jesus vicariously became "the great sinner" in Gethsemane (*The Power of*

*the Word: Saving Doctrines from the Book of Mormon* [Salt Lake City: Deseret Book, 1994], 13, 92, 178).

34. Robinson, *Believing Christ*, 118–19. Recent studies of the experiences of the Savior in Gethsemane can be found in Andrew C. Skinner, *Gethsemane* (Salt Lake City: Deseret Book, 2002) and Terry B. Ball, "Gethsemane," in *The Life and Teachings of Jesus Christ: The Savior's Final Hours*, ed. Thomas A. Wayment and Richard Neitzel Holzapfel (Salt Lake City: Deseret Book, 2003), 138–64.

35. The author of the Epistle to the Hebrews also taught that Jesus "was *in all points* tempted like as we are" (Hebrews 4:15; emphasis added).

36. Jeffrey R. Holland, "Special Witnesses of Christ," *Ensign*, April 2001, 14.

37. Elder Neal A. Maxwell explained Alma's prophecy: "Jesus also volunteered to take upon Himself *additional agony* in order that He might experience and thus know certain things 'according to the flesh,' namely *human sicknesses and infirmities and human griefs*, including those *not associated with sin*" ("Becoming a Disciple," *Ensign*, June 1996, 12; emphasis added).

38. The author of the Epistle to the Hebrews similarly taught that the Savior experienced these things "that he might be a merciful and faithful high priest in things pertaining to God, to make reconciliation for the sins of the people. For in that he himself hath suffered being tempted, *he is able to succor them that are tempted*" (Hebrews 2:17–18; emphasis added). It is significant that, following the completion of His experience in Gethsemane and Golgotha, the resurrected Savior declared to the Nephites: "I have

compassion upon you; my bowels are filled with mercy" (3 Nephi 17:7).
39. Neal A. Maxwell, "Enduring Well," *Ensign*, April 1997, 7; emphasis added.
40. Glenn L. Pace, "Crying with the Saints," *Ensign*, September 1988, 71. Elder Neal A. Maxwell also taught: "He [Christ] took upon Himself our sins as well as our pains, sicknesses, and infirmities. (See Alma 7:11–12.) Thus He knew, not in abstraction but in actuality, 'according to the flesh,' the whole of human suffering. He bore our infirmities before we bore them. He knows perfectly well how to succor us. We can tell Him nothing of pain, temptation, or affliction" (*We Will Prove Them Herewith* [Salt Lake City: Deseret Book, 1982], 46–47).
41. See also Mosiah 5:7: "Because of the covenant which ye have made ye shall be called *the children of Christ*, his sons, and his daughters; for behold, this day he hath spiritually begotten you; for ye say that your hearts are changed through faith on his name; therefore, ye are born of him and have become *his sons and his daughters*" (emphasis added).
42. The Hebrew verb "to see" (*ra'ah*) can mean literally "to see" with the eyes, or figuratively "to perceive" with the mind. See Francis Brown, S. R. Driver, and Charles A. Briggs, eds., *A Hebrew and English Lexicon of the Old Testament* (New York: Oxford University Press, 1951), 906–8.
43. Merrill J. Bateman, "The Power to Heal from Within," *Ensign*, May 1995, 14; emphasis added.
44. Neal A. Maxwell, *Plain and Precious Things* (Salt Lake City: Deseret Book, 1983), 43. Note also Elder Maxwell's

further teaching: "Jesus knows the sheep of His fold not only for *what they now are* but also for *what they have the power to become*" (*Even As I Am* [Salt Lake City: Deseret Book, 1982], 78.)

45. Note Elder Neal A. Maxwell's plea: "Do we understand—really comprehend—that Jesus knows and understands when we are stressed and perplexed? The complete consecration which effected the Atonement ensured Jesus' perfect empathy; He felt our very pains and afflictions before we did and knows how to succor us" ("Swallowed Up in the Will of the Father," *Ensign*, November 1995, 24). See also Neal A. Maxwell, *If Thou Endure It Well* (Salt Lake City: Bookcraft, 1996), 52; Robinson, *Believing Christ*, 122–23.

46. Richard Neitzel Holzapfel and David Rolph Seely, *My Father's House: Temple Worship and Symbolism in the New Testament* (Salt Lake City: Bookcraft, 1994), 60; see also Leviticus 16:14–15; Hebrews 9:7.

47. Neal A. Maxwell, *One More Strain of Praise* (Salt Lake City: Deseret Book, 1999), 40. In a previous book, Elder Maxwell taught: "Jesus knows and cares for each individual; He watches carefully over the seemingly smallest of things" (*That Ye May Believe* [Salt Lake City: Bookcraft, 1992], 205).

48. Gene R. Cook, "The Grace of the Lord," *New Era*, December 1988, 4.

49. Jeffrey R. Holland, "Broken Things to Mend," *Ensign*, May 2006, 70–71.

JENNIFER C. LANE

# Hostility toward Jesus: Prelude to the Passion

By the final Passover of Jesus's life, the plans had been laid for His death. Although He had evaded being captured or being discredited on previous trips to Jerusalem, efforts were now focused to bring closure to what the leaders by this time had convinced themselves was a dangerous threat to the people for whom they had responsibility. At this point the hostility of the elite had coalesced into a plan for action that was well known among the pilgrims coming to Jerusalem for the Passover festival: "And the Jews' passover was nigh at hand: and many went out of the country up to Jerusalem before the passover, to purify themselves. Then sought they for Jesus, and spake among themselves, as they stood in the temple, What think ye, that he will not come to the feast? Now both the chief

---

Jennifer C. Lane is an assistant professor of Religious Education at BYU–Hawaii.

priests and the Pharisees had given a commandment, that, if any man knew where he were, he should shew it, that they might take him" (John 11:55–57).

In our reading of the New Testament, we naturally assume this hostility toward Jesus is consistently found throughout all the Gospels. Here I would like to explore some of the background that helps explain why the Pharisees in particular had initial concerns about the Savior's actions and then how, over time, those concerns developed into hostility and defensiveness. Seeing how hostility and defensiveness develop in interactions with Jesus recorded in the New Testament can help us better understand the opposition the Savior faced from the leaders of the Jews in the last part of His life.

While we have more records of encounters between the Savior and the Pharisees than between the Savior and any other group in the New Testament, it is important to recognize that it was not the Pharisees who were solely responsible for the efforts to end the Savior's life. The chief priests and the Sadducees had their own religious and political concerns that led them to oppose Christ and develop hostility toward Him over time.

The Pharisees were split by different schools of thought, and those who lived in different areas were not directly connected to one another. Thus, interactions in Galilee may not have had an immediate influence on the feelings of those in Jerusalem.[1] In this paper I will, however, focus on the accounts of interactions between the Savior and the Pharisees with hope of clarifying how people seeking to be loyal to the truth may become hardened and hostile when they are challenged to rise to a higher level. In giving an in-depth look into one of the groups that were influential during the life of Jesus, I hope we can see a general pattern of righteous people deciding how to respond to a call to repent and become more holy.

In covenanting with the children of Israel, the Lord commanded, "Ye shall be holy; for I am holy" (Leviticus 11:44). The effort to seek holiness and separate themselves from the world around them was both a challenge and a source of identity for the Israelites throughout their history. This pursuit of holiness continued beyond Old Testament times, into the intertestamental era and the time of the Savior's mortal ministry. During the intertestamental period and the life of Jesus, hellenized culture pressured the Jews to leave the standards of the covenant. Their distinctiveness in diet, circumcision, and Sabbath-day observance were held up to ridicule. One small Jewish group that actively resisted this pressure was the Pharisees. Their efforts focused on ritual purity in food preparation and eating as well as careful observance of the Sabbath. Their strict efforts to live the law of Moses and bring the holiness of the temple into the lives of all the Jews grew out of this defensive position. In their efforts to find holiness, they also criticized others who did not keep their standards.

The New Testament accounts of the Pharisees' critique of the Savior and His followers can be better understood when seen in this historical context. Their beliefs about the nature of holiness help to explain their initial concerns about the Savior. When Jesus was criticized for His failure to follow the Pharisees' understanding of holiness, He responded to their critique with teachings that pointed to the true nature of holiness. Interestingly, He frequently used the words of Old Testament prophets to make His point, teaching that the divine nature of holiness had already been revealed. As He gave these rebukes to His critics, they were in a position to change their perspective and seek a higher form of holiness. But, as with all inspired chastisement, they were also free to harden their hearts and resist His teaching. As we shall see, for the Pharisees who debated with Jesus the general pattern was that of resisting the call to repentance. When these Pharisees refused to rethink what it meant to be holy, their defensiveness turned into hostility and fueled their active resistance to the Savior and His call to holiness.

## THE PHARISEES' VISION OF HOLINESS

The Pharisees' opposition to Jesus centered on critiques of food practices and Sabbath observance that went against their understanding of true Judaism. At the center of the Pharisees' concern was their confidence in what the Gospels refer to as "the traditions of the elders" (Matthew 15:2; Mark 7:5), also known as "ancestral tradition."[2] A central focus of the law of Moses concerned the sacrifices in the temple and the strict rules governing the ritual purity of the priests while they officiated and ate at the temple. While other Jews of this time believed that these regulations in Leviticus applied only to the priests in the temple, the Pharisees' goal was to bring the holiness of the temple into every home through applying these laws more broadly.

The Pharisees had recently developed a vision of what they believed the law of Moses meant for the holiness of all Jews. The Pharisees' revolutionary claim was that the ritual

## "Hostility toward Jesus: Prelude to the Passion"

temple holiness described in the law was God's will for all Jews, not just the priests.[3] All could obtain this holiness by eating "secular food (ordinary, everyday meals) in a state of ritual purity *as if one were a Temple priest*. The Pharisees thus arrogated to themselves—and to all Jews equally—the status of Temple priests."[4]

This desire to bring the purity and holiness of the temple into their homes meant that the Pharisees had to take very seriously a number of things associated with food and eating. It led the Pharisees to focus on the purification of vessels and the washing of hands to make the meals ritually pure. Ritual purity also explains their emphasis on tithes because for them proper tithing of food made the "food ritually acceptable."[5] To keep this level of holiness, it was also essential not to eat with those who did not observe these laws.[6] This combined effort to keep the ritual holiness of the family table is known as table fellowship. As we shall see, much of the Pharisees' initial opposition to Jesus arose over questions of His or His disciples' food practices, particularly as they reflected a breach of table-fellowship regulations. Their critique was that they were not following the standards of holiness.

When we see how the Pharisees sought to live exemplary lives in ordinary circumstances, we can better understand their concerns and see where their Achilles' heel lay. In the Sermon on the Mount, Jesus explained that the Pharisees' righteousness was a high bar that His followers had to surpass: "For I say unto you, That except your righteousness shall exceed the righteousness of the scribes and Pharisees, ye shall in no case enter into the kingdom of heaven" (Matthew 5:20). When we realize that the Pharisees were trying to live a holy life in a world they saw as unclean, we can better identify with their efforts to be righteous, as well as their efforts to justify or defend themselves. Recognizing that their efforts and even their initial opposition grew out of their desire for righteous lives, we more easily "liken them unto ourselves" (1 Nephi 19:23).

## CRITIQUES AND RESPONSES

Once we understand the Pharisees' vision of holiness, we can see why they would have had concerns about what they saw as lapses in Jesus's and the disciples' behavior, and we can better explain why they opposed it. As we examine the critiques of the Pharisees who are described in the Gospels and the Savior's responses in calling them to a higher level of holiness, we can see the escalation of resistance and hostility that eventually led them to seek His death.

The Pharisees' resistance to the call to rethink holiness helps to explain the source of their hostility to Jesus. It is also helpful to note that the Savior was challenging the Pharisees' role in interpreting the law. His challenge to their vision of ritual holiness surely could have provoked a hostile reaction as it threatened the social status of the Pharisees as the interpreters of the law. But while this context helps to explain pressures and motivations, the response of hostility is not, however, simply a political question. At its core, hostility reflects personal choices and spiritual responses. The hostility we find described in the Gospels was informed by a particular context, but, more

## "Hostility Toward Jesus: Prelude to the Passion"

importantly, it was a universal spiritual phenomenon—the "universal sin" of pride.

The pattern of questioning turning into hostility because of the Pharisees' defensiveness increasingly characterizes the hostile interactions of the Pharisees and the Savior. We'll look now at two concerns raised against Jesus: that He was eating with sinners and that He was eating with unwashed hands. We can see that these questions grew out of the Pharisees' understanding of the law of Moses. Their religious commitment to ritual purity put them in a position of opposition to what they saw Jesus and His disciples doing. In His responses to their questions, Jesus shows the Pharisees that scripture itself points to a higher form of holiness. In realizing that they are being told that their efforts at spiritual excellence are falling short, they are in a position where—depending on their response—they can be humbled or develop hostility.

*Eating with sinners.* New Testament accounts suggest that Jesus was invited to participate in the Pharisees' table fellowship (see Luke 11:37, Luke 14:1), but we also learn that others He ate with were an affront to the Pharisees. Understanding the concept of table fellowship helps us see that by eating with others that were ritually unclean Jesus would also threaten the purity of His Pharisaic hosts. The tax collectors, or publicans, were specifically excluded from the Pharisees' table fellowship.[7] In the first account of eating with publicans and sinners, we learn that the "scribes and Pharisees murmured against his disciples, saying, Why do ye eat and drink with publicans and sinners?" (Luke 5:30) or "Why eateth your Master with publicans and sinners?" (Matthew 9:11; see also Mark 2:16). For the Pharisees, those who keep the ritual cleanliness of the priests in their homes allow the holiness of the temple to reside in the home. But in order to keep this level of holiness, it was required that they eat only with others who were equally obedient.

The initial "murmuring" about eating with publicans and sinners is met with Jesus's teachings that the "whole need not a physician, but they that are sick" and "I am not come to call the righteous, but sinners to repentance" (Matthew 9:12–13; see also Mark 2:17; Luke 5:31–32). On its face it might not be clear how these comments would rile the "scribes and Pharisees" because they would naturally concur that the sinners and tax collectors were sick and did need a physician. They could see themselves as righteous and the others as unworthy. One of our greatest challenges as righteous, law-abiding people is to recognize that we all sin. To the extent that our observance of the law becomes our sense of justification before God, then admitting that we are flawed will not be an option. Then, at all costs, we must exactly keep the law and judge others who do not. In Matthew's account, the Savior points out this universal tendency in His accusers with an additional phrase that calls the questioners into question and invites them to a higher level of holiness.

In Matthew 9:13 we read that between the statements about the sick and His mission to call them to repentance, an additional comment is, "But go ye and learn what that meaneth, I will have mercy, and not sacrifice." This is a quotation from the prophet Hosea chastising the unrighteous Israelites: "O Ephraim, what shall I do unto thee? O Judah, what shall I do unto thee? for your goodness is as a morning cloud, and as the early dew it goeth away. For I desired mercy, and not sacrifice; and the knowledge of God more than burnt offerings. But they like men have transgressed the covenant: there have they dealt treacherously against me" (Hosea 6:4, 6–7).

Jesus is challenging the scribes' and Pharisees' interpretation of scripture in telling them, "Go ye and learn what that meaneth." Their understanding of holiness, which required strict adherence to the requirements for priests' ritual purity, had become for them "sacrifice" and "burnt offerings." Jesus is challenging their fundamental conception of holiness and the law by questioning their focus on their own ritual purity while ignoring the spiritually sick among the covenant people.

In using this quote from Hosea, Jesus suggests that His questioners, like the wicked Israelites, were misunderstanding God's will and the nature of God's holiness as they placed their self-justifying obedience over compassion for the less obedient. "For I desired mercy, and not sacrifice; and the knowledge of God more than burnt offerings" (Hosea 6:6). Imbedded in the context of the quote we find a prophetic critique of the ultimate lack of depth and staying power of self-justifying righteousness: "O Judah, what shall I do unto thee? for your goodness is as a morning cloud, and as the early dew it goeth away" (Hosea 6:4). While "by faith was the law of Moses given," Jesus is pointing here to "a more excellent way" (Ether 12:11), a kind of compassionate righteousness that exceeds "the righteousness of the scribes and Pharisees" (Matthew 5:20). He is pointing to a righteousness based on the mercy of God rather than the belief that we can be justified and saved by our own obedience to the law.

Another debate over the nature of holiness is found in the Pharisees' opposition to the Savior's table-fellowship practice and His subsequent questioning of the questioners in Luke 15. Here "the Pharisees and scribes murmured, saying, This man receiveth sinners, and eateth with them" (Luke 15:2). Jesus responds to their critique with the parable of the ninety-nine sheep that are safe and the one sheep that is lost in the wilderness. The imagery of a lost, vulnerable sheep replaces His earlier explanation of the sick needing a physician, but the challenge to the spiritual caretakers is the same. While their concern was based on their desire to maintain the table fellowship that would make their tables as holy as the altar of the temple, Jesus was, however, challenging them to look to an even higher vision of holiness. Just as Hosea had challenged the wicked Israelites to seek "the knowledge of God" rather than merely the temple worship of "burnt offerings" (Hosea 6:6), here Jesus challenges those spiritual leaders that would be holy by describing the nature of divine holiness seen in the imagery of God's care for His covenant people as shepherd (see Ezekiel 34:11–12, 16).

Jesus teaches the Pharisees who disapproved of eating with sinners that as contemporary spiritual leaders the Good Shepherd should be their model. His use of the parable of the ninety and nine suggests that in their focus on their own holiness in table fellowship, they are instead following the example of the ancient "shepherds of Israel" (Ezekiel 34:2) who, concerned with their own advantage, ignored those that were lost. The prophet Ezekiel had been commanded to "prophesy against the shepherds of Israel, prophesy, and say unto them, Thus saith the Lord

## "Hostility toward Jesus: Prelude to the Passion"

God unto the shepherds; Woe be to the shepherds of Israel that do feed themselves! should not the shepherds feed the flocks?" (Ezekiel 34:2). In this extended critique against the spiritual leaders of ancient times, the Lord tells them that they have ignored the lost sheep: "And they were scattered, because there is no shepherd: and they became meat to all the beasts of the field, when they were scattered. My sheep wandered through all the mountains, and upon every high hill: yea, my flock was scattered upon all the face of the earth, and none did search or seek after them" (Ezekiel 34:5–6). Those leaders set to represent God cared for themselves and not for those they could have helped. In comparing the lost sheep and the sinners who were in need of help, Jesus delivers a prophetic rebuke to the Pharisees who sought their own table-fellowship holiness by not eating with sinners.

This neglect of the lost is placed in direct contrast to the care given by Jehovah as the Good Shepherd: "For thus saith the Lord God; Behold, I, even I, will both search my sheep, and seek them out. As a shepherd seeketh out his flock in the day that he is among his sheep that are scattered; so will I seek out my sheep, and will deliver them out of all places where they have been scattered in the cloudy and dark day. . . . I will seek that which was lost, and bring again that which was driven away" (Ezekiel 34:11–12, 16). The holiness and goodness of the Good Shepherd was found in His loving care of those who were scattered and lost. Christ's rebuke against the contemporary "shepherds of Israel" carries with it an invitation to a higher way as He points to the true holiness of forgetting self and reaching out to the lost sinners. But, as with all spiritual correction, this response opens up the possibility of resentment and defensiveness in the hearer.[8]

*Not washing hands.* As the Gospel narratives proceed, an escalation in hostility to Jesus can be seen in the new questions raised by those among the Pharisees. In the earlier issue of eating with sinners, concerns were raised about His and His disciples' practice, but in these exchanges there was no immediate reaction to Jesus's calling the questioners' own holiness into question. When Pharisees begin to question Him about not washing hands, we see an escalation of hostility toward Jesus. In Matthew 15 and Mark 7, the question is put to Jesus why His disciples do not also follow "the tradition of the elders" in the washing of hands before eating (Matthew 15:2; Mark 7:3). The earlier comments about eating with publicans and sinners may have implied that these others' ritual uncleanness would diminish the holiness of Jesus and His disciples. In the challenge about not washing hands, they are being accused of not being holy by not living up to the Pharisaic interpretation of how to bring the temple's holiness to every house in Israel.

Christ responds to these accusers' question of holiness by taking on the issue of the authority of the "tradition of the elders" (Matthew 15:2; Mark 7:3). He first illustrates the problems in setting up something beyond the law by discussing how another practice sanctioned under their tradition can be a justification for not keeping the commandments of God (see Matthew 15:3–6; Mark 7:9–13).[9] He also quotes Isaiah's description of a hypocritical people and describes it as a prophecy of His accusers (see Matthew 15:7–9; Mark 7:6–8).

In the prophetic critique found in Isaiah 29:13, the Lord describes a people who appear to want holiness, but their hearts and their understanding are not right with God. The Lord speaks against those who "draw near me with their mouth, and with their lips do honour me, but have removed their heart far from me, and their fear toward me is taught by the precept of men" (Isaiah 29:13). It is not just the lack of correlation between hearts and words, but also "their fear toward me is taught by the precept of men." This fits directly into Jesus's questioning the authority of the "tradition of the elders" and in Mark precedes His very strong comment that "for laying aside the commandment of God, ye hold the tradition of men, as the washing of pots and cups: and many other such like things ye do. And he said unto them, Full well ye reject the commandment of God, that ye may keep your own tradition" (Mark 7:8–9). In the version of Isaiah that Jesus quotes, the critique on false worship is particularly strong: "But in vain they do worship me, teaching for doctrines the commandments of men" (Matthew 15:9; see also Mark 7:7).

In addition to this strong critique of the Pharisees' vision of holiness, the situation escalates as Jesus calls "the multitude" (Matthew 15:10) to Him and publicly teaches that being defiled or impure is not a matter of what we take into ourselves. Instead, our concern should be on what we produce: "Not that which goeth into the mouth defileth a man; but that which cometh out of the mouth, this defileth a man" (Matthew 15:11). In teaching this "more excellent way" (Ether 12:11), Jesus also directly and publicly refutes the authority and interpretation around which the Pharisees' understanding of holiness was built.

It is not surprising, then, that at the end of Jesus's commentary His disciples came "and said unto him, Knowest thou that the Pharisees were offended, after they heard this saying?" (Matthew 15:12). In listening defensively to Jesus's teaching on holiness, these Pharisees had ears to hear the rebuke but not the invitation.

A similar incident is recorded in Luke 11 in which the questioning of Jesus's practice is then turned around and He calls the Pharisees' vision of holiness into question. In this scene it is not the practice of the disciples, but of Jesus Himself that is challenged. "A certain Pharisee besought him to dine with him: and he went in, and sat down to meat. And when the Pharisee saw it, he marvelled that he had not first washed before dinner" (Luke 11:37–38). In response to this questioning of His breach of the "tradition of the elders," Jesus begins an extensive critique of the danger of disguising the inner self with outward righteousness. These comments touch on several practices associated with the Pharisees' program of holiness: "[making] clean the outside of the cup and the platter; but your inward part is full of ravening and wickedness" (Luke 11:39), being exacting in tithes, by "[tithing] mint and rue and all manner of herbs, and [passing] over judgment and the love of God" (Luke 11:42). It is, however, significant to note, as in Matthew 23 where similar critiques appear, that these comments are not framed as an attack on the Pharisees' practices, but rather focus on what they yet lack (see Matthew 19:20). Concerning "judgment and the love of God," Jesus says, "These ought ye to have done, and not to leave the other undone" (Luke 11:42). It is the sins of omission that become the barrier to true holiness.

As with the incident of conflict over eating with unwashed hands found in Matthew and Mark, this scene in which the Pharisees are chastised leads to heightened tension. Wanting so much to be holy, the Pharisees who were chastised did not want to hear that their efforts were misguided and were falling short. This would be an indictment of their entire way of life and their confidence of being justified before God through their righteous deeds. We learn that "as he said these things unto them, the scribes and the Pharisees began to urge him vehemently, and to provoke him to speak of many things: laying wait for him, and seeking to catch something out of his mouth, that they might accuse him" (Luke 11:53–54). In this defensive response to the Savior's call to repentance, we can see hostility developing among the Pharisees. The hope of those who spoke with Him to "wait for him" and catch Him saying something "that they might accuse him" came only "as he said these things unto them."

## RESISTING THE CALL TO HOLINESS

What is striking in the New Testament accounts is not that the Pharisees maintained religious or political opposition to Jesus but that some became hostile in that opposition. We have seen here how the Pharisees' initial concerns centered around ritual cleanliness, although the same pattern holds for their emphasis on the Sabbath day.

While the Pharisees' understanding of how to live the law of Moses led to their initial opposition to Jesus, it was not their focus on ritual purity that caused their negative feelings. Their hostility toward Jesus was neither earlier fixed as a part of their program, nor was it a given result of the experiences that they had with Him. Their opposition may have been a matter of different beliefs, but the hostility we see reflects the enmity and hardening of heart that grow from pride. This is a pattern that we can see throughout the scriptures and in our own lives.

The Pharisees lived in a time of great challenge for the covenant people. They had a vision of bringing the holiness of the temple into the lives of all the Jews and diligently set about living their lives in harmony with that vision. In this effort they believed that they were living genuinely holy lives. They were trying very hard to keep the highest standards they could. During His ministry the Savior pointed them to a higher level of holiness, portraying sinners not as those who pollute our ritual holiness but as the sick and lost sheep who need the care of those who are well. Hearing this vision of holiness which focused on meeting others' needs rather than merely rejoicing in their own righteousness, they began to recognize changes they could make. The choice was theirs, as it is all of ours, to repent or to harden our hearts. But choosing to resist the call to repent will lead us to increased hostility toward the One calling us to change.

Seeing the escalation of hostility throughout the Savior's ministry, it is not a great surprise when we read that, after the reports of the raising of Lazarus had reached

## "Hostility toward Jesus: Prelude to the Passion"

the Pharisees, "then gathered the chief priests and the Pharisees a council, and said, What do we? for this man doeth many miracles. If we let him thus alone, all men will believe on him: and the Romans shall come and take away both our place and nation" (John 11:47–48). The defensiveness and fear on the part of the leaders of the Jews is palpable in these statements. A pattern of resistance to the Savior's call had eventually developed a sense of Jesus as a threat in the minds of many of the elite.

We can see that the feeling of being threatened became formulated in political terms by the last months of Jesus's ministry. It is not clear from the historical evidence that the Romans did see Jesus as a threat, but it is important to understand the pressures that the elite of the Jews were under. They were an occupied people, ruled by the Romans in Judea and a Roman supported ruler in Galilee. Although each of the different Jewish groups had found varying strategies of negotiating the political and social pressures of Roman rule and hellenization, it was in nobody's interest to lose what political and religious autonomy they had. This sense of shared threat can help explain why the chief priests and Pharisees were working together to solve what they saw as a shared problem. It may or may not have been an accurate fear, but it was understandable in light of the fragile political situation they faced.

The prophetic statement of the high priest Caiaphas, who unknowingly testified of the Atonement, was also a clear statement of their feeling of justification: "It is expedient for us, that one man should die for the people, and that the whole nation perish not" (John 11:49–50). The subtle escalation of hostility from offense at being challenged and rebuked had grown to the point at which they associated not just their own well-being but also the survival of their nation on eliminating this threat. By the last months of Jesus's life, the defensiveness of the political and religious elite had led them to feel justified in working toward His demise: "Then from that day forth they took counsel together for to put him to death" (John 11:53).

While these leaders have sometimes been portrayed as evil incarnate, their feelings of defensiveness and resistance may be closer to home than we would like. Those who responded defensively sought to protect themselves from the Savior's critique and call to a higher level of holiness. Surely, they thought, we are right and He is wrong. We are living a holy life. We are keeping the commandments. In their hostility we see, as in a mirror, our own response to chastisement as pride rather than humility. Hostility becomes our defense when we resist the call to repentance.

## NOTES

1. Many of the interactions between Jesus and the Pharisees took place in Galilee, and the Pharisees involved in working for His death were in Jerusalem. While it is not fully clear what relations existed between the different groups interacting with Christ at different times, I believe that the pattern of response we see with the texts we have can give us insights into a broader sense of how hostility developed in those who saw Jesus as their enemy.
2. Martin S. Jaffee, *Early Judaism* (Upper Saddle River, NJ: Prentice-Hall, 1997), 79. Jaffee states, "But what does seem certain—because it is the only thing upon which

our otherwise irreconcilable sources agree—is that the Pharisees placed a great premium on something called 'ancestral tradition.'" All sources consistently assent to the Pharisees' focus on "ancestral tradition" that the rabbis would later call the oral law.

3. See Jacob Neusner, *From Politics to Piety: The Emergence of Pharisaic Judaism* (Englewood Cliffs, NJ: Prentice-Hall, 1973), 83.
4. Neusner, *From Politics to Piety*, 83; emphasis in original.
5. Neusner, *From Politics to Piety*, 80.
6. "Pharisees furthermore ate only with other Pharisees, to be sure that the laws were appropriately observed" (Neusner, *From Politics to Piety*, 80).
7. Neusner, *From Politics to Piety*, 73.
8. An important examination of the role of defensiveness and resentment in hardening hearts can be found in Terry Warner, *Bonds That Make Us Free: Healing Our Relationships, Coming to Ourselves* (Salt Lake City: Shadow Mountain, 2001).
9. For background on the practice of corban, see Max Wilcox, "Corban," in *The Anchor Bible Dictionary*, ed. David Noel Freedman (New York: Doubleday, 1992), 1:1134; and "Corban" in *The International Standard Bible Encyclopedia*, ed. Geoffrey Bromily (Grand Rapids, MI: Eerdmans, 1979), 1:772.

JOHN W. WELCH

# The Legal Cause of Action against Jesus in John 18:29–30

People have long questioned why Jesus was executed. Was He put to death by Romans or by Jews? Was it on political charges or for religious offenses? Were the proceedings legal or illegal? Answers to such questions have proven extremely evasive and have generated a vast body of scholarly analysis and amateur literature[1] because the trial of Jesus is extremely complicated legally. It is one of the most difficult and controversial legal subjects in the history of the world. Thus, caution is in order whenever one embarks on the study of this topic.

In this chapter, I will focus on only one aspect of the trial of Jesus as recorded in John 18:29–30. The accusation in those verses holds a key for understanding the legal cause of action and strategy of the chief priests

---

John W. Welch is a law professor at the J. Reuben Clark Law School at Brigham Young University.

before Pilate in the proceedings against Jesus. The focus here is only on John 18:29–30; this is not an attempt to give a complete account of the entire episode.²

## HISTORICAL BACKGROUND

Many legal issues immediately confront anyone approaching the trial of Jesus, but none is more fundamental than determining which legal rules applied to such a case in Jerusalem in the early decades of the first century. Consider, for example, the commonly asserted prohibition that Jewish trials could not be conducted at night. This rule is found in the Talmud, but the Talmud was not written until many years after the destruction of Jerusalem—a generation after the death of Jesus. Moreover, the Talmud was written by the religious descendants of the Pharisees and thus represents the views of the Pharisees. In first-century Jerusalem, however, the Pharisees and the Sadducees disagreed on many legal technicalities, and it is unknown what the Sadducees thought about trials at night. It is unclear whether the Sadducees, the lay nobility who were the leaders of the Sanhedrin,³ would have had any legal objections to a nighttime arrest, hearing, and conviction. Similar legal problems are encountered at just about every turn in pondering the Jewish and Roman trials of Jesus.

Several factual perplexities also hinder our understanding. For example, was the trial actually held at night? It is clear that Jesus was arrested at night, but perhaps that happened well into the night and near the predawn hours. Luke, in fact, says that it was day before

## "The Legal Cause of Action against Jesus"

the trials actually began (see Luke 22:66), although it must have been very early in the morning, since many things happened between the time Jesus was arrested and when He was taken to Golgotha about nine in the morning (see Mark 15:25). It is worth noting that it was customary among the Romans to be at work before daybreak, but without knowing when the trial actually began or ended, it is hard to know whether the rule against nighttime trials was violated, even assuming that there was a prevailing law against such proceedings at the time of Jesus.

Moreover, verbal ambiguities make legal analysis in many cases quite difficult. For instance, Jesus is accused of "deceiving" the people. Does this mean that His accusers thought He fooled them maliciously, carelessly, or perhaps even unwittingly? Did they think that He was deceptively encouraging them to commit sin or erroneously teaching them to think incorrectly or tricking them into apostasy? Did they think that His deception was simple antisocial misrepresentation, or was it illegal fraud? Without knowing more about what His accusers meant, it is hard to know why they thought His words or doings were deceptive in a way that warranted the death penalty.

But most of all, how could the general concerns of the chief priests and the Romans have been translated into a specific legal cause of action against Jesus?[4] Was He accused of blasphemy? Yes (see Matthew 26:65–66; Mark 14:63–64), but there must have been more to the case than this (in ancient trials, legal causes of action were often added one on top of the other). If blasphemy alone had been the issue, one would expect that Jesus would have been stoned by the Jews,[5] which was the biblically prescribed mode of execution for blasphemy (see Leviticus 24:16; Acts 6:11; 7:59). And because Pilate and the Romans would have cared very little about a Jewish accusation of blasphemy, scholars have often concluded that Jesus must have been executed for some other reason, perhaps on charges of treason against Rome, since He was accused of having called Himself the king of the Jews and this appellation ended up on the placard placed by Pilate above Jesus on the cross. But it is very hard to see any substance to a claim of treason against Jesus. He was an unarmed pacifist, a Galilean peasant who said, "All they that take the sword shall perish with the sword" (Matthew 26:52). When asked by Pilate about His kingship, Jesus answered, "My kingdom is not of this world" (John 18:36). From his response, it appears that Pilate was satisfied that Jesus posed little, if any, threat to Rome or to the Emperor Tiberius: "I find in him no fault" (John 18:38). Such considerations lead to the persistent question, what might have been the main legal cause of action that carried the most weight against Jesus and led to His crucifixion?

## A MALEFACTOR

A solution to this problem is in the Gospel of John. All readers of the New Testament must choose between either relying primarily on John and then secondarily on the synoptics to fill in the gaps, or relying primarily on the synoptics and then secondarily on John. I prefer the former because John's report makes impeccable legal sense, and John can be trusted as a witness of these proceedings. He was one of the leading Apostles, along with Peter and

## "The Legal Cause of Action against Jesus"

James. John was at Golgotha and would have known as much as possible about what was happening and why. John 18:15 tells us that "another disciple . . . went in" to Annas's house. Was this Judas? Or Nicodemus? More likely, it was the Apostle John himself, who was thus an eyewitness of these legal proceedings. While the Gospel of John is the most theological of the Gospels, it is also in many ways the most authentic historically; John's account is especially in touch with Jesus's Galilean and Jewish background.

John 18:29–30 most significantly reports the verbal exchange between Pilate and the chief priests as they brought Jesus to the Praetorium: "Pilate then went out unto them, and said, What accusation bring ye against this man? They answered and said unto him, If he were not a *malefactor,* we would not have delivered him up unto thee" (emphasis added). What did the chief priests mean by "malefactor"? Here lies the key to understanding the legal cause of action that they lodged against Jesus as they brought Him to Pilate.

A bit of background becomes important here, for the English word *malefactor* is the translation of the Greek work *kakopoios,* which (like its closely related Latin word, *maleficus*) in legal contexts can mean "magician" or "sorcerer." To understand how ancient people generally, and the leaders of the Jewish establishment in particular, would have reacted to Jesus and His miracles, modern readers must understand the positive and negative attitudes of ancient Jews and Romans toward magic. In certain cases, both Jews and Romans had strict laws that punished magicians, sorcerers, fortune-tellers, diviners, those in contact with spirits, and miracle workers.

Most relevant to the trial of Jesus is the biblical law that makes it a capital offense to use miracles (signs or wonders) to lead people into apostasy (to go after other gods): "If there arise among you a prophet, or a dreamer of dreams, and giveth thee a sign or a wonder, and the sign or the wonder come to pass, whereof he spake unto thee, saying, Let us go after other gods, . . . that prophet, or that dreamer of dreams, shall be put to death" (Deuteronomy 13:1–2, 5; compare also Leviticus 20:27). Of course, Jewish law recognized that there were good uses of supernatural powers as well as bad. Jewish attitudes toward magic were mixed. Witness the contest between Pharaoh's magicians and Moses. King Saul visited the witch of Endor, but Exodus 22:18 commands, "Thou shalt not suffer a witch [either male or female] to live." The Jews took magic seriously enough that one of the qualifications to be a member of the Sanhedrin was the ability to differentiate good miracle working from trafficking with evil spirits.[6]

Equally interesting is the fact that Roman law also proscribed certain uses of magic and divination. Empire-wide decrees adopted in AD 11 and 16, during Jesus's own lifetime, elevated suspicions and sensitivities about rogues or irregular invocations of supernatural powers. Roman law and society at that time considered magicians, along with brigands, pirates, astrologers, philosophers, and prophets, as enemies of the Roman order. For these people, gods both good and evil were everywhere; thus, unseen spirits and demons were taken seriously as a constant potential threat. Especially when combined with *maiestas* (anything that insulted, suborned, or threatened the emperor), condoning any such use of supernatural powers would

"The Legal Cause of Action against Jesus"

easily make a person an enemy of Caesar (see John 19:12). Here is a Roman concern that the chief priests could have waved before Pilate to try to capture his attention.

### MIRACLE WORKING

All this becomes relevant to the trial of Jesus in light of His miracle working. Above all, it seems clear that miracle working got Jesus in a great deal of trouble with those Jewish leaders who rejected Him. We know that He never used His power to harm anyone, but people at the time did not know where He would stop. If Jesus could still the storm, then He could cause earthquakes (the most likely way the temple could be instantly destroyed), and His words to this effect were alleged (however wrongly) as a serious threat to the temple: "We heard him say, I will destroy this temple" (Mark 14:58).

Legal debates had in fact ensued over the miracles of Jesus. People wondered by whose power He did His miracles (see Acts 4:7). In Mark 3:22, scribes (legal officials) were brought all the way to Galilee from Jerusalem to give their legal opinion in this case. Their determination was that "He hath Beelzebub [Satan], and by the prince of the devils casteth he out devils." There was not a theological debate going on, then, but a legal investigation resulting in an allegation with dire legal implications.

This same debate continued in Jerusalem. In John 10:19–21, we learn that "there was a division therefore again among the Jews for these sayings. And many of them said, He hath a devil, and is mad; why hear ye him? Others said, These are not the words of him that hath a devil. Can a devil open the eyes of the blind?"

As Jesus came to Jerusalem for the very last time, one final miracle tipped the scales against Him—the raising of Lazarus. A miracle of this magnitude and notoriety, performed in Bethany just over the hill from the temple in Jerusalem, raised legal issues that could not be ignored. After this miracle, "from that day forth they took counsel together for to put him to death" (John 11:53). The equivalent of a warrant for the arrest of Jesus was issued: "Now both the chief priests and the Pharisees had given a commandment [a legal order], that, if any man knew where he were, he should shew it, that they might take him" (John 11:57). And it should be noted that Lazarus was also listed as a wanted man: "The chief priests consulted that they might put Lazarus also to death; because that by reason of him many of the Jews went away, and believed on Jesus" (John 12:10–11). In the chief priests' minds, Lazarus too was leading people into apostasy by colluding with Jesus.

With this background and clear development of factors in the Gospel of John, it is hard to imagine how Jesus's miracle working would not have been the dominant factor that galvanized the chief priests against Him. However, while laws against sorcery are mentioned occasionally by commentators writing about the trial of Jesus, this underlying concern or cause of action is not usually given much attention by readers or scholars. It seems to me that the main reason for this disregard is that no formal accusation of magic, or *maleficium*, ever appears to be made in the three synoptic Gospels. But in light of the foregoing discussion, a closer look at John 18:30 is required.

### "The Legal Cause of Action against Jesus"

Recognizing that a term such as *maleficus*, *kakopoios*, or *kakon poion* should be understood in a general sense meaning "criminal," "save where it is qualified to take on a specific meaning,"[7] here are ten reasons why the word *malefactor* in John 18:30 is qualified to take on a technical legal reading ("magician" or "sorcerer").[8] These linguistic or circumstantial reasons give grounds upon which I conclude that the legal cause of action brought by the chief priests against Jesus as they ushered Him into Pilate's chamber was that He was an illegal miracle worker or magician, using illicit powers to threaten the public order, both Roman and Jewish:

*The legal setting.* Ordinary words carry technical, legal import when used in a judicial context. English words such as *action*, *motion*, *bench*, and *arise* all have regular meanings in ordinary speech, but they assume a legal meaning when they are spoken in court, as is the case here.

*The legal request.* When Pilate asked, "What sort of accusation do you bring against this man?" he was not saying, "What's going on here?" His words call for a specific legal response. He would expect the petitioners to formulate their words back to him in terms of cognizable causes of action under Roman law.

*The logic of the exchange.* In the synoptic Gospels (of which John was presumably aware), Pilate was said to have asked, "What [*kakon*] has he done?" (Matthew 27:23; Mark 15:14; Luke 23:22). In their discourse with Pilate, if John were to have the chief priests simply respond, "Oh, he was doing *kakon*," their response would be circular, evasive, and probably insulting. Their answer is best understood as being more specific than simply a repetition of the question back to the magistrate.

*The strong meaning of the word.* Many astrological treatises, magical papyri, and other documents use the word *kakopoios* to describe bad mystical agents. In an emotionally charged setting, such as the hearing before Pilate, speakers or writers typically do not use strong words in a weak sense.

*A legal characterization of early Christians.* The early Christians themselves were seen by others as being involved in magic. Suetonius states that Christians in the first century were accused of being involved in *"superstitionis novae ac maleficae,"*[9] a label that implies charges of magic.

*Contemporaneous legal prosecution of other miracle workers.* Apollonius, who coincidentally was raised in Tarsus about the same time as was Saul, was another miracle worker in the first century after Christ. He was "tried for his life by Domitian," who accused Apollonius "of divination by magic for Nerva's benefit," among other things. Apollonius's emphasis "on supernatural revelations inevitably led to his being accused of magical practices" on other occasions as well.[10]

*Exorcism and wonder working.* Jesus and His disciples were indisputably depicted as exorcists, the implications of which have been quite thoroughly explored in other contexts.[11] But even exorcism used for improper purposes in an open and notorious fashion would have produced legal trouble. Carl Kraeling has argued persuasively that people generally said of Jesus that He "has a demon," meaning that He "has a demon under his control," a concept commonly applied in the ambient culture to people having

"The Legal Cause of Action against Jesus"

access to the "spirits of persons [such as John the Baptist] who had died a violent death."[12] After Jesus healed a man with a withered hand on the Sabbath and was then accused by people in the synagogue, He asked them, "Is it lawful to do good on the sabbath days, or to do evil [*kakopoiēsai*]," and His accusers "held their peace" (Mark 3:4). Obviously, it was not lawful to do evil, magical works on any day.

*Use in 1 Peter.* The only other place where the word *kakopoios* appears in the New Testament is in two passages in Peter's first epistle, where it likely refers "to an individual guilty of legally defined crimes."[13] Peter wrote that people generally were talking about Christians as "evil makers," but he is confident that judges and others will see their good works, glorify God, and pronounce them not "evil makers" but "good makers" (see 1 Peter 2:12, 14). Here the label of "evil makers" was intended by outsiders to be deeply insulting, not weakly pejorative. Even more definitively, in 1 Peter 4:13–16, Christians were exhorted to share the suffering of Christ, but not as a murderer, a thief, a *kakopoios*, or as a fourth kind of offender (the nature of which is more general and indeterminable). Clustered together with the first two very serious offenses in this list, the word *kakopoios* points to a particular crime of unacceptable magnitude.

*Early Christian attestations.* Some early Christians, such as Lactantius in the late third or early fourth century, openly acknowledged that the Jews had accused Jesus of being a magician or sorcerer.[14] Christians did not answer by arguing that this word in John 18:30 should be understood in some weak sense. They answered by arguing that the miracles of Jesus were acceptable because the prophets had predicted them.

*Confirmations from early Jewish sources.* Evidence of Jewish opinion at the time of Lactantius is the following passage from the Babylonian Talmud, tractate Sanhedrin 43a: "On the eve of the Passover Yeshu [the Nazarine] was hanged. For forty days before the execution took place, a herald went forth and cried, 'He is going forth to be stoned because he has practiced sorcery and enticed Israel to apostasy. Any one who can say anything in his favor, let him come forward and plead on his behalf.' But since nothing was brought forward in his favor he was hanged on the eve of the Passover."

Ultimately, however, Pilate found no such cause of action against Jesus and so held, "I find in him no fault," or in other words, "I recognize no legal cause of action against him" (John 18:38; author's translation). Pilate was satisfied that Jesus of Nazareth had not broken any Roman law, though others saw Jesus's use of miraculous powers as a threat of treason or sedition. Nevertheless, Pilate was apparently still fearful enough about the situation that he was willing to permit or take some action.

## EARLY DEPICTIONS OF CHRIST

All of this is corroborated by the fact that Jesus's role as a miracle worker and wonder worker was a dominant part of His public reputation in the first and second centuries. This is evident from the writings of Josephus, both in Greek and Slavonic. For example, the Slavonic Josephus states:

## "The Legal Cause of Action against Jesus"

"And [Pilate] had that Wonder-worker brought up, and after instituting an inquiry concerning him, he pronounced judgment: 'He is [a benefactor, not] a malefactor, [nor] a rebel, [nor] covetous of kingship.' [And he let him go; for he had healed his dying wife.]"[15]

The earliest extant Christian art offers further witness of the popular reputation that Jesus had as a wonder worker, not only among His detractors, but also His followers. Pre-Constantinian images of Jesus depict Him as a miracle worker more often than in any other pose. The most common compositional element of these images shows Jesus holding a magic wand with which He performs His supernatural feats. It would be hundreds of years after the death of Christ before the cross or the Passion narratives became the main subjects of Christian art. Instead, the raising of Lazarus (see John 11:1–43), the raising of Jairus's daughter (see Mark 5:22–43; Luke 8:41–56), the miracles of loaves and fishes (see Mark 6:38–44; 8:5–19; Matthew 14:17–19; 15:34–36; Luke 16:9–10; John 6:9–13), and the turning of water into wine (see John 2:1–11) were the most popular narratives depicted in the first few centuries.[16] As one scholar has noted, "To such Christians the life of Christ consisted simply of a series of miracles."[17] And in depicting these miracles, Jesus touches the body of the deceased, the loaf-filled baskets, and the water-filled amphora with His magic wand. Although found in several locations, the majority of these images are found in the Christian funerary sculpture and painting in the Roman catacombs—a twelve-mile underground labyrinth of niches, alcoves, and passageways beneath Rome. Here, graves were often decorated with religious motifs, sometimes quite elaborately. The resurrection of the deceased was metaphorically promised by miraculous scenes such as the miracles of Christ, Jonah and the whale, and the deliverance of Shadrach, Meshach, and Abednego from the fiery furnace.

Ancient artists added the detail of Jesus holding a wand to the Gospel miracle stories because of the popular correlation of a wand with magicians. In Homer's *Odyssey*, for example, Circe—the magician daughter of Helios—is depicted working her magic with a wand when she transforms a group of people into pigs. In Roman mythology, Mercury was one of the gods who escorted souls to and from the afterlife. Just as Mercury is depicted holding his golden wand to lead the dead back to life, Jesus too is shown magically bringing people back to life with a wand or staff.[18]

## CONCLUSION

One may wonder why the fearful factor of magic has not been emphasized previously in scholarly or religious literature about the trial of Jesus. I would suggest at least three main reasons.

First, few scholars want to allow that the miracles of Jesus really happened. If they did not happen, of course, they could not have been a factor in the historical trials of Jesus before the Sanhedrin and Pilate. But if they did happen, it is hard to see how they could have failed to be

## "THE LEGAL CAUSE OF ACTION AGAINST JESUS"

a dominant factor in the case of the chief priests against Jesus of Nazareth.

Second, Christians today generally do not want to associate Jesus with magic or with any suggestion that He was a trickster. But the line between good miracles and bad magic is definable by their results. Jesus Himself said, "By their fruits ye shall know them" (Matthew 7:20) and asked, "How can Satan cast out Satan? And if a kingdom be divided against itself, that kingdom cannot stand" (Mark 3:23–24). Christians should celebrate, not obfuscate, the miracles of Jesus.

Third, critical scholars generally give more historical weight to the accounts in Matthew, Mark, and Luke than in John. But in light of the fact that all three of the synoptic Gospels report that Pilate asked, "What [*kakon*] has he done?" (see Matthew 27:23; Mark 15:14; Luke 23:22), the formulation by the chief priests of the legal cause of action against Jesus in John 18:30 becomes all the more significant. The charge that Jesus was a *kakopoios* (a *malificus*, or magician, wonder worker) raises an issue that both Jews and Romans would take seriously.

Of course, it would help if the world accepted the Book of Mormon, which long ago revealed that even after all His mighty miracles "they shall consider him a man, *and say that he hath a devil*, and shall scourge him, and shall crucify him" (Mosiah 3:9; emphasis added). It seems to me, as the Book of Mormon makes quite clear, that these miracles lead to Jesus's scourging and crucifixion. His mighty miracles forced the issue then—and now—of identifying by what power did Jesus do these things. If He did them by the power of God, then He should be accepted and followed; but if He did them by the power of Beelzebub, then He should be feared and eliminated.

Jesus certainly came with power. He was the Creator of the world—good enough, wise enough, and powerful enough to bring to pass the salvation, immortality, and eternal life of all mankind. If He could raise Lazarus from the dead, He could control many other situations of life and death in this world and in the world to come. His powers were also sufficiently in control of all that needed to happen as He came into this world and as He went out of it (see John 10:18). He came to win the cosmic battle against death and hell, to engage the powers of evil, to drive out devils from paralytics and demoniacs, and to cast out Satan eternally. How could He do all of this and *not* find Himself accused of dealing with the realms of the paranormal?

NOTES

1. For an extensive listing of scholarly sources, see John W. Welch, *Biblical Law Cumulative Bibliography*, CD-ROM (Winona Lake, IN and Provo, UT: Eisenbrauns and Brigham Young University Press, 2005).

2. For a more complete and fully footnoted treatment, see John W. Welch, "Miracles, *Maleficium*, and *Maiestas* in the Trial of Jesus," in *Jesus and Archaeology*, ed. James H. Charlesworth (Grand Rapids, MI: Eerdmans, 2006), 349–83. A version of that paper focusing on biblical, Jewish, and Roman laws regarding magic was presented at the Biblical Law Section of the Society of Biblical Literature, annual meeting, November 2005.

3. See Joachim Jeremias, *Jerusalem in the Time of Jesus: An Investigation into Economic and Social Conditions during the New Testament Period* (Philadelphia: Fortress, 1969), 229, 265.
4. People ordinarily assume that the actions against Jesus were based on some colorable legal grounds and were not just strokes of arbitrary discretion.
5. In John 18:31, the Jews say to Pilate that they lack the authority to execute anyone. It is possible that the Jews were just being careful and deferential toward Pilate, or perhaps even a bit disingenuous, hoping that he would take responsibility for executing Jesus. New Testament evidence (as in the attempts to stone Jesus in Nazareth or the incident of the woman taken in adultery) shows that on some occasions the Jews had or took power to put people to death. In the case of Jesus, the Jews eventually received a release from Pilate to do with Jesus as they pleased (see John 19:16), which—if blasphemy were the only issue—would normally have entailed stoning. But since they urged Pilate to crucify Jesus, the execution went forward in that manner.
6. b. Sanhedrin 17a. See also Welch, "Miracles, *Maleficium*, and *Maiestas* in the Trial of Jesus," 366.
7. Graham H. Twelftree, *Jesus the Exorcist: A Contribution to the Study of the Historical Jesus* (Peabody, MA: Hendrickson, 1993), 204.
8. These reasons are detailed and footnoted in Welch, "Miracles, *Maleficium*, and *Maiestas* in the Trial of Jesus."
9. Suetonius, *de Vita Caesarum*, 6.16 (Nero).

10. Frederick H. Cramer, *Astrology in Roman Law and Politics* (Philadelphia: The American Philosophical Society, 1954), 222–23.
11. See Morton Smith, *Jesus the Magician: Charlatan or Son of God?* (Berkeley: Seastone, 1998); Robert J. Shirock Jr., "Whose Exorcists Are They: The Referents of Hoi Yhioi Hymn at Matthew 12:17/Luke 11:19," in *Journal for the Study of the New Testament*, no. 46 (1992): 41–51; and C. K. Barrett, *The Holy Spirit and the Gospel Tradition* (London: SPCK, 1947), chapter 4.
12. Carl H. Kraeling, "Was Jesus Accused of Necromancy?" *JBL* 59 (1940): 153–57.
13. John H. Elliott, *1 Peter: A New Translation with Introduction and Commentary*, The Anchor Bible (New York: Doubleday, 2000), 468. When Luke calls the two other criminals crucified with Jesus "malefactors" (Luke 23:32), the Greek word he uses is *kakourgos*, not *kakopoios*. Luke's word refers to "robbers," and it must mean something different to Luke than *kakopoios* means to John, or else we must imagine that the Jews in John 18:30 were accusing Jesus of being a "robber," an allegation that lacks any plausible basis.
14. See Lactantius, *Divine Institutes*, 5, 3; in *Patrologia Latina* 6.560–61.
15. Josephus, *The Jewish War Books IV–VII*, trans. H. St. J. Thackeray (Cambridge: Harvard University Press, 1928), 648–50; brackets in this translated source.
16. See Thomas F. Mathews, *The Clash of Gods: A Reinterpretation of Early Christian Art*, rev. ed. (Princeton, NJ: Princeton University Press, 1993), 54–91; and Robin Margaret Jensen, *Understanding Early Christian Art* (New York: Routledge, 2000), 64–93.

## "The Legal Cause of Action against Jesus"

17. Mathews, *Clash of Gods*, 59.
18. See Mathews, *The Clash of Gods*, 58–59. In the note appended to his text, Mathews cites the following sources as evidence of the use of a wand. For Circe, he cites Homer, *Odyssey*, 10.293, 388; Virgil, *Aenid*, 7.189–91; Ovid, *Metamorphoses*, 14.278, 413. For Mercury, he cites Homer, *Odyssey*, 24.1; Virgil, *Aenid*, 4.242; Prudentius, *Contra Symmachum*, 1.89–91. I thank Josh E. Probert for his research on early Christian art.

RICHARD E. BENNETT

# "It Is Finished": The Divine Accomplishment of the Crucifixion

Him, being delivered by the determinate counsel and foreknowledge of God, ye have taken, and by wicked hands have crucified and slain. (Acts 2:23)[1]

At this sacred Easter season of the year, between the Good Friday of Christ's death and the Sunday of His Resurrection, it is fitting to meditate upon the life, mission, and particularly the death and sacrifice of our Lord and Savior, Jesus Christ. This is a most sacred topic, surely one of the mysteries of godliness, or as William W. Phelps's oft-sung hymn puts it, "that sacred, holy off'ring, by man least understood."[2] President Gordon B. Hinckley has said, "No member of this Church must ever forget the terrible price paid by our Redeemer,

---

Richard E. Bennett is a professor of Church history and doctrine at Brigham Young University.

CELEBRATING EASTER

. . . the agony of Gethsemane, the bitter mockery of His trial, the vicious crown of thorns tearing at His flesh, . . . the terrifying pain as great nails pierced His hands and feet. . . . We cannot forget that. We must never forget it, for here our Savior, our Redeemer, the Son of God, gave Himself, a vicarious sacrifice for each of us."[3] The great Protestant Reformer Martin Luther once said: "Whoever meditates thus upon God's sufferings for a day, an hour, yea, for a quarter of an hour, we wish to say freely and publicly, that it is better than if he fasts a whole year, prays the Psalter every day, yea, than if he hears a hundred masses. For such a meditation changes a man's character and almost as in baptism he is born again, anew."[4]

The specific purpose of this chapter is to ponder on the suffering and death of Jesus Christ, to consider Gethsemane and the Crucifixion of the Son of God, and that to understand such divine drama was an ordained accomplishment. While everything about the life and death of Christ was foreordained and prepared "from the foundation of the world" (Moses 7:47)—as Pope Benedict XVI has said, "The Cross of Jesus is a cosmic event" and "Nothing is mere coincidence; everything that happens is contained in the Word of God and sustained by his divine plan"[5]—we will look only at the final chapter of a perfect, sinless life and show that Christ was not the hapless victim of evil circumstance but the supreme architect of a perfect Atonement.[6] It was, in the words of scripture, if not a miracle, then certainly a divine accomplishment, a "high commission to fulfill."[7]

## "The Divine Accomplishment of the Crucifixion"

The Crucifixion was an accomplishment in that from the Mount of Transfiguration to Golgotha, Christ left little, if anything, to chance. It was an accomplishment in that His Crucifixion fulfilled prophecy in every particular detail and occurred just as He taught and predicted it would occur. It was an accomplishment in that evil men, in exercising their agency to condemn the Son of God, were fully responsible for their own sins. As President Hinckley has written, "He loves us so much that He shed drops of blood in Gethsemane, then *permitted* evil and wicked men to take Him, to compel Him to carry the cross to Golgotha, to suffer beyond any power of description terrible pain when He was nailed to the cross, to be lifted up on the cross, and to die for each of us."[8]

It was also an accomplishment in that Christ successfully took upon Himself the sins of all mankind, thereby obeying every word of His Father in Heaven. In the final week of Christ's life, commonly referred to as the Passion Week, while men mocked and devils laughed, the master of deception was blinded by his own deceit. The central redeeming act of Christ's mortal ministry and of man's immortality and eternal life, made necessary because of Adam's transgression, could no more have been left to chance than could the earth have been accidentally created. It was, in every way, a fulfillment of the plan of salvation as laid out before this world was created. As the Apostle Peter came to understand and express so poignantly, "Him, being delivered by the *determinate counsel and foreknowledge of God*, ye have taken, and by wicked hands have crucified and slain" (Acts 2:23; emphasis added).

Celebrating Easter

Pondering upon such things is the very core of lasting personal testimony and conversion. Wrote the Apostle Paul, "But we preach Christ crucified, unto the Jews a stumbling block, and unto the Greeks foolishness" (1 Corinthians 1:23). And again, "For I determined not to know any thing among you, save Jesus Christ, and him crucified" (1 Corinthians 2:2). Modern revelation indicates that one of the abiding gifts of the Holy Spirit is not only to "know that Jesus Christ is the Son of God," but also *"that he was crucified for the sins of the world"* (D&C 46:13; emphasis added). Indeed, the Doctrine and Covenants is replete with references to the Crucifixion and our understanding of it as Jesus bears witness anew of His long-ago sacrifice. It confirms repeatedly the fact that "he came into the world, even Jesus," for this very moment, "to be crucified for the world, and to bear the sins of the world, and to sanctify the world, and to cleanse it from all unrighteousness" (D&C 76:41). For, He said, "I am Jesus Christ, the Son of God, who was crucified for the sins of the world, even as many as will believe on my name" (D&C 35:2).[9] And again to the Prophet Joseph F. Smith: "Redemption had been wrought through the sacrifice of the Son of God upon the cross" (D&C 138:35).

"AND SPAKE OF HIS DECEASE"

Some six months before His death, Moses and Elijah appeared as translated beings before Christ on the Mount of Transfiguration. In Peter's words, they heard the voice of God the Father there declare, "'This is my beloved Son, in whom I am well pleased" (2 Peter 1:17). Among the many

## "THE DIVINE ACCOMPLISHMENT OF THE CRUCIFIXION"

other important things said and done on this majestic occasion, Moses and Elijah also "spake of his [Christ's] decease which he should accomplish at Jerusalem" (Luke 9:31). A moment of glorification, the Transfiguration was also a time of preparation and review of what the prophets of old had long said concerning Christ's death and of what must inevitably transpire on Christ's final walk to Calvary. Elder James E. Talmage has said of it, "We may safely assume that the time was devoted, in part at least, to the further instruction of the Twelve respecting the rapidly approaching consummation of the Savior's mission on earth, the awful circumstances of which the apostles were loath to believe possible."[10] Also, as Elder David B. Haight has more recently said, "He went up to prepare for His coming death. He took His three apostles with Him in the belief that they, after having seen His glory—the glory of the Only Begotten of the Father—might be fortified, that their faith might be strengthened to prepare them for the insults and humiliating events which were to follow."[11]

And all along the way, He taught His disciples in all of the particulars pertaining to His pending demise, though He was careful not to agitate them to the point of interfering with His mission. The very next day after the Transfiguration, "when they were come down from the hill," He said to His disciples, "Let these sayings sink down into your ears: for the Son of man shall be delivered into the hands of men. But they understood not this saying, and it was hid from them, that they perceived it not" (Luke 9:37, 44–45).[12]

And with ever-increasing clarity as the time of His death drew closer, Christ continued to prophesy and expound upon these things to followers who could not, or would not, understand. Mark indicates, "He taught his disciples, and said unto them, the Son of man is delivered into the hands of men, and they shall kill him; and after that he is killed, he shall rise the third day. But they understood not that saying, and were afraid to ask Him" (Mark 9:31–32). While going up to Jerusalem, Jesus "took again the twelve, and began to tell them what things should happen unto him, Saying, Behold, we go up to Jerusalem; and the Son of man shall be delivered unto the chief priests, and unto the scribes; and they shall condemn him to death, and shall deliver him to the Gentiles: and they shall mock him, and shall scourge him, and shall spit upon him, and shall kill him: and the third day he shall rise again" (Mark 10:32–34). Matthew further points out another essential detail—that He knew beforehand and taught He "shall be betrayed unto the chief priests and unto the scribes" (Matthew 20:18). Thus, Christ knew well the culture, environment, and details pertaining to His pending death.

## "WHEN IT TESTIFIED BEFOREHAND THE SUFFERINGS OF CHRIST"

One also wonders if His disciples comprehended the plenitude of prophecies that He was about to fulfill. Only later did Peter, filled with the Holy Ghost, come to realize the magnitude of what had happened as he declared, "Of which salvation the prophets have enquired and searched diligently, who prophesied of the grace that should come unto you: searching what, or what manner of time the Spirit of Christ which was in them did signify, when it testified beforehand the sufferings of Christ, and the glory that should follow" (1 Peter 1:10–11).

The Crucifixion, and every lamentable element leading up to it, would occur in such a way as to fulfill a multitude of ancient prophecies. Christ, the God of the Old Testament, knew long before His coming what manner of death He would suffer; He revealed such to His ancient prophets. Enoch saw in a vision the ignominious manner of Christ's Crucifixion, for Jehovah said unto Enoch: "Look," and Enoch "beheld the Son of Man lifted up on the cross, after the manner of men" (Moses 7:55). Enoch also said, "The Righteous is lifted up, and the Lamb is slain from the foundation of the world; and through faith I am in the bosom of the Father" (Moses 7:47).

Nephi, a Book of Mormon prophet, understood not only how the Messiah would be crucified but also who would be responsible. "It must needs be expedient," Nephi prophesied, "that Christ . . . should come among the Jews, among those who are the more wicked part of the world; and they shall crucify him—for thus it behooveth our God, and there is none other nation on earth that would crucify their God" (2 Nephi 10:3).[13] The Apostle Paul likewise wrote of Christ and His death: "Which none of the princes of this world knew: for had they known it, they would not have crucified the Lord of glory" (1 Corinthians 2:8).

Nephi also saw the many degrading details of the events leading up to the Crucifixion. "And the world, because of their iniquity, shall judge him to be a thing of naught; wherefore they scourge him, and he suffereth it; and they smite him, and he suffereth it. Yea, they spit upon him, and he suffereth it. . . . And the God of our fathers

... yieldeth himself ... into the hands of wicked men, to be lifted up ... and to be crucified ... and to be buried in a sepulchre" (1 Nephi 19:9–10). In the Old Testament, Isaiah prophesied as follows: "But he was wounded for our transgressions, he was bruised for our iniquities: the chastisement of our peace was upon him; and with his stripes we are healed ... and the Lord hath laid on him the iniquity of us all" (Isaiah 53:5–6; see Mosiah 14:5–8).

And in one of the great messianic prophecies of the Old Testament, the Psalmist captured many of the final details attending Christ's death on Calvary:

> But I am a worm, and no man; a reproach of men, and despised of the people.
>
> All they that see me laugh me to scorn: they shoot out the lip, they shake the head, saying,
>
> He trusted on the Lord that he would deliver him: let him deliver him, seeing he delighted in him. . . .
>
> I am poured out like water, and all my bones are out of joint: my heart is like wax; it is melted in the midst of my bowels.
>
> My strength is dried up like a potsherd. . . . They pierced my hands and my feet. . . . They look and stare upon me.
>
> They part my garments among them, and cast lots upon my vesture. (Psalms 22:6–8, 14–18)

David even recorded some of the very words Christ would utter from the cross: "My God, my God, why hast thou forsaken me?" (Psalm 22:1; see also Matthew 27:46). As one scholar has so aptly phrased it, "None of

## "The Divine Accomplishment of the Crucifixion"

this suffering was unforeseen; it was all part of the plan of salvation from before the world was created."[14]

If the Apostles could scarcely comprehend these things beforehand, the Savior's enemies were even more resolutely blind to them. Peter was among the very first to see the awful irony that only after Christ's death, and only after he, Peter, had received the gift of the Holy Ghost, whose mission it is to "teach . . . all things" and to "bring all things to [our] remembrance," did Peter comprehend fully both who his master really was, what Christ had accomplished, and by what powerful means (John 14:26). "For of a truth against thy holy child Jesus, whom thou hast anointed," a much wiser Peter later prayed to his Father in Heaven, "the people of Israel were gathered together, for to do whatsoever thy hand and thy counsel determined before to be done" (Acts 4:27–28). Clarifying still further, Peter went on to explain to the Jewish leaders their unwitting participation. "And now, brethren, I wot [know] that through ignorance ye did it, as did also your rulers. But those things which God before had shewed by the mouth of all his prophets, that Christ should suffer, he hath so fulfilled" (Acts 3:17–18). In other words, Peter was boldly declaring to them that in their very act of denying and crucifying Christ, they were exercising their agency to condemn themselves while fulfilling prophecy. In modern scripture, Christ revealed again this truth. For "the Comforter . . . manifesteth that Jesus was crucified by sinful men for the sins of the world, yea, for the remission of sins unto the contrite heart" (D&C 21:9). While preaching in Antioch, the Apostle Paul demonstrated that he also understood these truths: "For they that dwell at Jerusalem, and their rulers, because they knew him not, nor yet the voices of the prophets which are read every sabbath day, *they have fulfilled them in condemning him*. And though they found no cause of death in him, yet desired they Pilate that he should be slain. And when they had fulfilled all that was written of him, they took him down from the tree, and laid him in a sepulchre" (Acts 13:27–29; emphasis added). Likewise Nephi bore record of this terrible truth of wickedness fulfilling righteousness when he wrote, "But because of priestcrafts and iniquities, they at Jerusalem will stiffen their necks against him, that he be crucified" (2 Nephi 10:5).

Clearly Christ was master of His own destiny. Knowing all things from the beginning, He knew He would have to enter into Jerusalem at the feast of the Passover; that so great an uproar must erupt in Jerusalem as to cause Roman interference; that Satan would enter into Judas, one of His own, who would then betray Him (see Luke 22:3); that evil men, full of jealousy and rage, envy and deceit, would betray and condemn Him and in so doing bring down judgment upon their heads; that He must die in full public view, at the hands of Roman guards outside the city and before the Passover upon a cross between two thieves; and finally, that He would die in such a way as to mask the fact that He gave his life, though it would appear to all that it was taken from Him.

## THE ROAD TO CALVARY

How, then, would all such things be accomplished? Surely Christ knew that He would not escape His final

## "The Divine Accomplishment of the Crucifixion"

entry into Jerusalem and that men would seek His life at almost every turn. The raising of Lazarus from the dead in Bethany just before Christ's coming to Jerusalem was a miracle bound to stir up the countryside, or as the scriptures put it, "The people also met him, for that they heard that he had done this miracle" (John 12:18). Since Lazarus's death was well known, his return from the dead led many faithful Jews to worship Christ while driving the Pharisees to jealousy. "Behold, the world is gone after him," they bitterly complained (John 12:19). Such attention would lead only to jealousy on the part of those Jewish leaders who "from that day forth . . . took counsel together for to put him to death" (John 11:53)—not only Christ but Lazarus as well (see John 12:10)—so as to blunt the rising tide of Jewish belief in the Man of Nazareth. Murder was ever in their hearts, and they sought every which way to accomplish their ends!

Six days before the Passover, as Jesus entered the city, "very great" and adoring crowds spread branches of palm trees in His pathway and cried, "Hosanna: Blessed is the King of Israel that cometh in the name of the Lord" (Matthew 21:8; John 12:13). Even in this moment of worship, Christ "[knew] all things that should come upon him" (John 18:4) and was heard to say, "And I, if I be lifted up from the earth, will draw all men unto me" (John 12:32).

Once inside the city walls, Christ pursued a deliberately powerful, majestic course of action aimed at fulfilling His objectives. He consecrated His Father's house, the temple, by driving out the money changers (see Matthew 21:12) and by healing within it the blind and the lame, both of which actions caused an uproar of praise and adoration on the one hand and criticism and derision on the other. For when the chief priests saw it, "they were sore displeased" (Matthew 21:15). Then turning His attention to Pharisees, Sadducees, and the other Jewish leaders, in both parable and forthright language, He boldly castigated them time and time again for their spiritual blindness, wickedness, and hypocrisy. "But woe unto you, scribes and Pharisees, hypocrites! for ye shut up the kingdom of heaven . . . ye devour widows' houses . . . and have omitted the weightier matters of the law. . . . ye are like unto whited sepulchres. . . . Ye serpents, ye generation of vipers, how can ye escape the damnation of hell?" (Matthew 23:13–14, 23, 27, 33). Such deserved condemnations, Jesus well knew, would hardly endear Him to those men increasingly desperate to "lay hands on him" and to put Him away; nevertheless, they "feared" doing so only because of the adoring multitude (Matthew 21:46).

Not content merely to chastise the corrupt Jewish leaders, Christ then charged them, or at least their ancestors, with the ancient murder of Zacharias, son of Barachias, "whom ye slew between the temple and the altar" (Matthew 23:35).[15] Stunned by His courage, stung by His accusations, and fearful that their grip on power was in terrible jeopardy, the "chief priests, and the scribes, and the elders of the people" assembled at the palace of Caiaphas "and consulted that they might take Jesus by subtilty [cunning] and kill him" (Matthew 26:3–4).

Much has been written on all sides about God's foreknowledge of what these evil men would do. Was

## "The Divine Accomplishment of the Crucifixion"

God the author of evil? Did He originate their sin and absolve them in the doing? Were they predestined to do the will of Satan? It seems clear that God's foreknowledge could not deprive man of his responsibility. As Matthew recorded, "Woe unto the world because of offences! for it must needs be that offences come; but woe to that man by whom the offence cometh!" (Matthew 18:7). No amount of prophecy, no amount of planning, and no amount of God's foreknowledge could absolve that terrible sin of crucifying the Savior of the world. Only He could do that. Instead of being the author of sin, Christ is the finisher of our redemption.

Meanwhile Christ set forth on another, much quieter course of action—the Last Supper, in which He instituted the sacrament to replace forever the old Passover: "And he took bread, and gave thanks, and brake it, and gave unto them, saying, This is my body which is given for you" (Luke 22:19). When asked by His disciples where they should gather for this, their last meeting together, Jesus directed Peter and John to go into the city and "there shall a man meet you, bearing a pitcher of water; follow him" and "say unto the goodman ... Where is the guest chamber ... ? And he shall show you a large upper room furnished" (Luke 22:10–12). It is humbling to behold how in both this and the earlier obtaining of the colt or ass upon which He rode into the city, Christ knew precisely how to accomplish His designs and how to act upon the agency of men. These small acts, both prophecies fulfilled, well show that if He could foresee and accomplish such little things,

Christ could not have found anything pertaining to His mission beyond His grasp.

In His great intercessory prayers offered first at the Last Supper and later in Gethsemane, where He bled from every pore for the sins of all mankind, Christ spoke to His Father in Heaven in ways and of truths that are beyond mortal comprehension. One may grasp the fact that here, in a moment of agony when an angel appeared to render Him comfort, He wondered if this cup could be removed from Him: "Nevertheless not as I will, but as thou wilt" (Matthew 26:39). There is no stronger witness of Christ's willing obedience to the Father's will than Gethsemane and the cross. It appears, moreover, that Christ understood He had accomplished much of what He had been reminded of on the Mount of Transfiguration and that He was in the throes of fulfilling the mission of His life: "I have glorified thee on the earth: I have finished the work which thou gavest me to do. And now, O Father, glorify thou me with thine own self with the glory which I had with thee before the world was" (John 17:4–5).[16]

Any effort to artificially separate Gethsemane from the Crucifixion and from the subsequent Resurrection is futile. Christ's sacrifice and Atonement encompassed all three. As Elder McConkie aptly put it, "That which began in Gethsemane was finished on the cross and crowned in the resurrection."[17]

Then from Gethsemane to the cross: His betrayal, the uproar before Pilate, His appearance before Herod and return to Pilate, the agitation of the crowds to "Crucify him!" Pilate's reluctant decree to release the murderer Barabbas, the tortuous walk to Golgotha, the casting of lots for His robe, the driving of the nails into His hands and feet, and His being lifted up for all to see—all show that all these things were done to fulfill prophecy, to condemn unrighteousness, and to accomplish His death in the way He alone determined. For it was critical in the plan of heaven that Christ not be murdered on the sly, out of the way in a dark corner or blind alley, for the very fact that He could not be killed without His consent. His life was His to give, not one to be taken. While the scriptures do attest that He was "slain," His death, after six hours upon the cross, came only with His consent (see Luke 9:22; Acts 13:28; 1 Nephi 10:11). Christ's death, as President Joseph Fielding Smith has indicated, was "a voluntary act," not a murder but rather a willing sacrifice: "I lay down my life for the sheep . . . that I might take it again. No man taketh it from me, but I lay it down of myself. I have power to lay it down. . . . This commandment have I received of my Father" (John 10: 15, 17–18).[18]

Both prophecy and God's future purposes were fulfilled in the very method of the Crucifixion. The acts of pounding nails or spikes into the flesh of His hands and feet and piercing His side left wounds which will stand as lasting tokens of His death and Resurrection. Zechariah prophesied, "What are these wounds in thine hands? Then he shall answer, Those with which I was wounded in the house of my friends" (Zechariah 13:6). In this dispensation, Christ revealed to the Prophet Joseph Smith how such wounds will yet play a part in Christ's millennial return: "Then shall they know that I am the Lord; for I will say unto them: These wounds are the wounds with which I was wounded in the house of my friends" (D&C 45:52).[19]

## Celebrating Easter

In excruciating agony, alone upon the cross, stripped of all dignity and apparent power, and suffering not for Himself but for all mankind, Christ knew "that all things were now accomplished" (John 19:28). He then prayed to His Father, "Father, into thy hands I commend my spirit" (Luke 23:46). As John records, the Lord's dying words were, "It is finished: and he bowed his head, and gave up the ghost" (John 19:30). To the amazement of the Roman guards below who were accustomed to seeing men suffer for several hours, if not days, Christ died of His own volition. "The actual death of Jesus," wrote Talmage, "appeared to all who were present to be a miracle, as in fact it was."[20] Eliza R. Snow has written in her beautiful hymn "Behold, The Great Redeemer Die":

> He died, and at the awful sight
> The sun in shame withdrew its light!
> Earth trembled, and all nature sighed,
> In dread response, A God has died.[21]

One would grossly err in reducing the Crucifixion to the simple equation of prophecy fulfilled and promises realized. Though all this is true, it was infinitely removed from a mere mechanical or clever culmination. The enormous sinfulness of the act, Christ's incomprehensible suffering, and the very death of God defy all understanding. Elder Talmage writes: "It seems, that in addition to the fearful suffering incident to crucifixion, the agony of Gethsemane had recurred, intensified beyond human power to endure. In that bitterest hour the dying Christ was alone, alone in most terrible reality. That the supreme sacrifice of the Son might be consummated in all its fulness,

## "The Divine Accomplishment of the Crucifixion"

the Father seems to have withdrawn the support of His immediate Presence, leaving to the Savior of men the glory of complete victory over the forces of sin and death."²² The New Testament speaks of an earthquake (see Matthew 27:54) and three hours of gross darkness in Palestine. The Book of Mormon tells of three days of thick darkness and terrible destructions upon all the face of the land in the Americas (see 3 Nephi 8:20). Enoch prophesied that upon Christ's death "the heavens were veiled; and all the creations of God mourned; and the earth groaned" (Moses 7:56). The prophet Zenos also prophesied, "And the rocks of the earth must rend; and because of the groanings of the earth, many of the kings of the isles of the sea shall be wrought upon by the Spirit of God, to exclaim: The God of nature suffers" (1 Nephi 19:12). Christ's death upon the cross triggered frightening natural catastrophes, especially on the American continent and on the isles of the sea, and may stand as the most frightful moment of all time.

Our purpose has been to show that in the walk from the Mount of Transfiguration through Gethsemane and finally to Golgotha, Christ left nothing to chance. He was careful to prepare His disciples for that which must occur. He was careful to fulfill all prophecy. He was careful in allowing evil men to work their wrath upon Him. And He was careful that His death came as a sacrifice. In all this, He accomplished all that His Heavenly Father desired of Him.

Just as Jesus Christ took upon Himself the sins of all mankind, so must every accountable human being take upon himself or herself His sacrifice. The Crucifixion is not just a spectacle to behold on our way out of Jerusalem or a mere historical fact to pore over and analyze. Ultimately, it must become an integral, if not the essential, experience of our lives. We may live because He died and was resurrected on the third day. His Atonement is as intimate as it is infinite, as personal as it is universal.[23] Though it is not part of our experienced memory, it must ever be engraved upon our minds and hearts and the very center of our souls.

## NOTES

1. The author wishes to thank Chontal Green and Arran Wytinck for their very capable assistance in researching materials for this chapter.
2. "O God the Eternal Father," *Hymns* (Salt Lake City: The Church of Jesus Christ of Latter-day Saints, 1985), no. 175.
3. Gordon B. Hinckley, "The Symbol of Our Faith," *Ensign*, April 2005, 4.
4. Martin Luther, "The True and the False View of Christ's Sufferings," in *Sermons of Martin Luther*, ed. John Nicholas Lenker (Grand Rapids, MI: Baker Book House, 1988), 188.
5. Cardinal Joseph Ratzinger, "Way of the Cross," (mediations and prayers given at the Good Friday 2005 celebration of the Office for the Liturgical Celebrations of the Supreme Pontiff, Presented March 22, 2005), http://www.catholicnewsagency.com.
6. The Reverend Robert C. Harbach has said it very well: "God is never put into a predicament; and the Cross was no afterthought, suddenly brought in to cope with an unforeseen difficulty. Nor was the death of Christ a calamity which calls for man's sympathy and pity.

Neither was his death a mere experiment, uncertain in its results.... It was perfectly planned in the eternal purpose and counsel of the sovereign God.... Christ was not a victim of circumstances" (Robert C. Harbach, "Christ's Predetermined Death," in *Reformed Witness* 8, no. 4 [April 2000], http://www.hopeprc.org/reformedwitness/2000/RW200004.htm).

7. "Behold, The Great Redeemer Die," *Hymns*, no. 191.
8. Gordon B. Hinckley, *Teachings of Gordon B. Hinckley* (Salt Lake City: Deseret Book, 1997), 29; emphasis added.
9. See D&C 20:23; 21:9; 45:52; 46:13; 53:2; 54:1. It may be surprising to some how often Christ refers to His Crucifixion in modern revelation.
10. James E. Talmage, *Jesus the Christ* (Salt Lake City: The Church of Jesus Christ of Latter-day Saints, 1981), 370.
11. David B. Haight, "We Beheld His Glory," *Ensign*, May 1977, 7. Elder Haight says further: "Though difficult for us to understand, Jesus himself must have been strengthened and sustained by Moses and Elijah to prepare Him for the suffering and agony ahead for Him in working out the infinite and eternal atonement of all mankind."
12. Mark tells us that Christ had been teaching the same to His disciples even before the Mount of Transfiguration experience (see Mark 8:31).
13. It should be understood that these and other scriptures are condemning of the Jewish leaders, not the Jewish people generally. "The primary instigators of the plot to kill the Savior were the Jewish *religious leaders* ... not the Jewish people as a whole, and not even all of the leaders, were the ones who plotted Jesus' death" (Gerald N. Lund, *Jesus Christ, Key to the Plan of Salvation* [Salt Lake City:

Deseret Book, 1991], 31–32). Further to this point, Elder Bruce R. McConkie has written: "We must not generalize to the point of assuming there were none among the Jews who knew and understood the mission and ministry of the Anointed One.... [He] was known and recognized and worshipped by many of his Jewish kinsmen while he yet dwelt among them.... It was Jewish converts ... who welcomed crucifixion and death rather than bring dishonor to the Messianic name that they as Christians chose to bear. Whatever we may say of the Messianic hopes and knowledge of the generality of the Jews, the basic reality remains unchanged that there were those [Jews] who believed" (Bruce R. McConkie, *The Mortal Messiah: From Bethlehem to Calvary* [Salt Lake City: Deseret Book, 1981], 1:46–47).

14. Paul Y. Hoskisson, "The Witness for Christ in Psalm 22" in *Covenants, Prophecies and Hymns of the Old Testament: The 30th Annual Sidney B. Sperry Symposium* (Salt Lake City: Deseret Book, 2001), 291. Elder Bruce R. McConkie, a careful student of all these things, has written: "We cannot believe that all these sayings—given as allusions, as similitudes, and in plain words—constituted a tithe, or a hundredth, or a thousandth part of what the Blessed One said of his coming death and crucifixion and of his resurrection on the third day. Nor can we think that the people generally were unaware of his teachings; friends and foes alike had fixed in their minds that such was his announced course. That few truly envisioned the import and glory of it all, there is no doubt" (*Mortal Messiah: From Bethlehem to Calvary*, 4:11).

## "The Divine Accomplishment of the Crucifixion"

15. It is probable that Jesus was referring to the murder of Zacharias mentioned in 2 Chronicles 24:20–22—the last murder mentioned in the Old Testament. Joseph Smith, in referring to this episode, condemned the Jewish leaders further for not teaching the truth far sooner. "Hence as they possessed greater privileges than any other generation, not only pertaining to themselves, but to their dead, their sin was greater, as they not only neglected their own salvation but that of their progenitors" (*Teachings of the Prophet Joseph Smith*, comp. Joseph Fielding Smith [Salt Lake City: Deseret Book, 1976], 222–23).

16. "Gethsemane," in the words of Vaughn J. Featherstone, "was the most severe experience of pain, suffering, and mental agony ever experienced. The demands physically, mentally, and spiritually were incomparable to any ever known in eternity" (*The Incomparable Christ: Our Master and Model* [Salt Lake City: Deseret Book, 1995], 80).

17. McConkie, *Mortal Messiah*, 224. While many Latter-day Saints tend to focus more on Christ's suffering in the garden of Gethsemane than they do on His crucifixion on Calvary, apostles old and new have pointed to the inseparability of the two in the accomplishment of Christ's perfect Atonement. To emphasize one at the expense of the other is to do a doctrinal disservice. Robert L. Millet has recently written: "We seem to have begun to place a greater stress upon Gethsemane than upon the cross. It is difficult to define exactly when this began to occur, although President Joseph Fielding Smith seems to have formalized this emphasis more than anyone. That it did occur is obvious to most of us who were raised in the Church; we were taught that Gethsemane, not the

cross, was where Jesus suffered for our sins and that as horrendous as would have been the pain of Golgotha, yet the suffering in Gethsemane was greater and more far-reaching. As time has passed, however, the leaders of the Church have begun to speak of the importance of both Gethsemane and the cross to emphasize that what began in Gethsemane was completed in Golgotha" (Robert L. Millet, "Where Did the Cross Go?" unpublished manuscript to Religious Education faculty, September 16, 2005, 16). Gerald N. Lund has further said of this: "We cannot possibly argue which portion of Christ's ministry is the most significant, for each aspect of his mission is an integral part of the whole design. It would be safe to say, however, that the events connected with the Last Supper, the Garden of Gethsemane, his arrest and trial, his crucifixion, and his resurrection were the culminating events of his ministry. From the day of his birth and through every step of his ministry, his face was set toward Jerusalem, the cross, and the empty tomb" (*Jesus Christ, Key to the Plan of Salvation*, 29–30).

18. Joseph Fielding Smith, *Doctrines of Salvation: Sermons and Writings of Joseph Fielding Smith*, comp. Bruce R. McConkie (Salt Lake City: Bookcraft, 1954), 1:127.

19. The Lamb of God would also have to be sacrificed in perfect similitude to animal sacrifices that had from Adam's day for centuries to follow characterized the atonement offering in the tabernacles of ancient Israel. A perfect male lamb, without blemish, would have to be sacrificed with no bones broken. Said the Lord: "And he gave unto them [Adam and Eve] commandments, that they should worship the Lord their God, and should offer

the firstlings of their flocks, for an offering unto the Lord. And Adam was obedient unto the commandments of the Lord. . . . And then the angel spake, saying: This thing is a similitude of the sacrifice of the Only Begotten of the Father, which is full of grace and truth" (Moses 5:5, 7); see also Joseph Fielding Smith, *Doctrines of Salvation*, 1:22–23.
20. Talmage, *Jesus the Christ*, 663.
21. "Behold, The Great Redeemer Die," *Hymns*, no. 191.
22. Talmage, *Jesus the Christ*, 661; see also McConkie, *Mortal Messiah*, 4:230.
23. See Merrill J. Bateman, "The Power to Heal from Within," *Ensign*, May 1995, 14.

KEITH J. WILSON

# THE CHRISTIAN HISTORY AND DEVELOPMENT OF EASTER

During the past four decades, President Gordon B. Hinckley has addressed the Church on a great variety of topics. One theme that he has repeatedly taught and emphasized is the Resurrection of the Lord Jesus Christ. Three times during the last twelve years alone he has centered his remarks in general conference on this miracle and its importance. In each of these talks, he employed lofty superlatives to emphasize the significance of Christ's Resurrection. In 1994 he referred to it as "the greatest miracle in human history." Two years later he called it "the greatest victory of all time." And then in 1999 he declared it to be "the greatest event in human history."[1] The prophet wants us to know that nothing can

---

Keith J. Wilson is an associate professor of ancient scripture at Brigham Young University.

approach the significance of this transcendent event that occurred some two thousand years ago. This chapter will trace the development of Easter as a religious celebration and will then discuss the Latter-day Saint observance and perception of Easter.

The prelude to the Easter celebration might best be traced from the onset of the Savior's mortal ministry, even though His death and Resurrection were certainly foreordained (Revelation 13:8, "The Lamb slain from the foundation of the world"). As soon as His earthly ministry commenced, Jesus began to point toward His death and Resurrection. John highlighted Jesus's first prediction of His sacrifice and Resurrection. Jesus had cleansed the temple of the money changers, after which a contingent of defiant Jews had challenged His authority and power by asking Him for a sign. His metaphoric response—"Destroy this temple, and in three days I will raise it up" (John 2:19)—must have left them wondering. The Jews misinterpreted His comment as if it referred to Herod's monumental temple. John, however, parenthetically inserted that Jesus's disciples remembered this prediction later after He had risen from the dead and had shown them His body. So from John we receive a very early reference to the anticipated Easter event.

As the ministry of Jesus unfolded, so did His predictions of His death and Resurrection. Matthew records that during His Galilean teaching Jesus fielded questions about signs twice (see Matthew 12:39–45; 16:1–4). He answered His inquirers that no sign would be given to unbelievers except the sign that was given to Jonah of three days in darkness. Not long after this, He told His disciples twice that the Son of Man—a prophetic circumlocution that was unclear to some of those who heard it—would be killed and raised again on the third day (see Matthew 16:21–22; 17:22–23). At the Mount of Transfiguration, heavenly messengers spoke to Jesus "of his death, and also his resurrection" (Joseph Smith Translation, Luke 9:31). John recorded that following the Feast of the Tabernacles, Jesus said that the Father loved the Son because He offered His own life and that He had power to take it up again (see John 10:17–18). All these predictions preceded the final week of Jesus's life and directed His believers toward the quintessential Easter morning. Yet these predictions were neither comprehensive nor comprehended by all.

A few weeks before His Resurrection, Jesus prefigured that miraculous moment. In a highly publicized miracle, Jesus raised a friend from death and commanded that friend, Lazarus, to leave his tomb. During the process He declared to all assembled, "I am the resurrection and the life" (John 11:25). The miracle had a magnetic effect upon His followers so that when Jesus later entered Jerusalem they flocked to see Him. Once again He taught them of His imminent death and Resurrection after three days (see Matthew 20:19). And finally, after the Last Supper, the Lord reminded His disciples that though He would be smitten He would rise again. Although Peter presumably faltered during the difficult hours of Jesus's trial, it seems apparent that he and the other disciples were repeatedly taught of Jesus's death and Resurrection. The first Easter did not occur unannounced.

And yet when Easter morning dawned, the believers appear to have been stunned by the reality or timing of the Resurrection. Both John and Luke record that as the disciples encountered the risen Lord or evidence of His Resurrection they resisted emotionally. Jesus's rebuke to them was pointed: "O fools, and slow of heart to believe all that the prophets have spoken: ought not Christ to have suffered these things, and to enter into his glory?" (Luke 24:25–26). As He revealed Himself to them and "their eyes were opened" (Luke 24:31), He commissioned them to carry forward the glorious news of that first Easter with the words, "As my Father hath sent me, even so send I you" (John 20:21). In another passage He proclaimed: "Thus it behoved Christ to suffer, and to rise from the dead the third day. . . . And ye are witnesses of these things" (Luke 24:46, 48).

So the event and the moment of Easter became the singular message of early Christianity. Luke highlighted this message as he commenced his account of the Acts of the Apostles. He wrote, "To [the Apostles] also he showed himself alive after his passion by many infallible proofs, being seen of them forty days, and speaking of the things pertaining to the kingdom of God" (Acts 1:3). Then Luke quoted the risen Lord directly as He charged His disciples to "be witnesses unto me both in Jerusalem . . . and unto the uttermost part of the earth" (v. 8). These disciples heeded His commandment and boldly went forth proclaiming Jesus Christ and the Easter message.

First were Peter, James, and John; they were followed later by Matthias, Paul, Barnabas, and others. Their messages were both bold and powerful, centering on the death and Resurrection of Jesus Christ (see Acts 4:29, 33). Paul the Apostle possessed perhaps the most commanding voice among them, and he ardently defended the Easter message. In his first letter to the Corinthian Saints, Paul defended the Resurrection in what is now the fifteenth chapter of Corinthians. He began with the words, "I declare unto you the gospel . . . that Christ died for our sins according to the scriptures; and that he was buried, and that he rose again the third day" (1 Corinthians 15:1, 3–4). He buttressed his claim with the fact that the Twelve, in addition to five hundred other brethren, saw the risen Lord. Then he reversed the tables in his argument and pressed the notion that without the Resurrection there is no gospel of Jesus Christ, no faith, no hope, no future. He concluded his treatise with his witness of the Resurrection, the defeat of death, and the great "victory through our Lord Jesus Christ" (1 Corinthians 15:57). From the writing and preaching of the early Apostles, the centrality of Christ's Resurrection became the doctrinal center of nascent Christianity.

## THE FORMATION OF EASTER AS A RELIGIOUS HOLIDAY

It comes as no surprise, then, that the early Christian Church developed many traditions and celebrations to commemorate this central event of that first Easter morning. Even though the first historical mention of Easter as an annual event did not occur until the late second century,[2] there is evidence from the New Testament that the early Apostles shifted their Sabbath from the seventh day to the first day of the week to commemorate the Resurrection on a weekly basis. Both John and Luke note that Christ's followers met together on "the first day of the week" (John 20:19; Acts 20:7; see also John 20:26). Luke also adds that the disciples were there to "break bread." The reason for the abrupt shift seems to be the miraculous Resurrection; each Sabbath day for those earliest Christians was either a commemoration of or a reflection on the Easter miracle. Early Christian apologists Justin Martyr and Tertullian corroborate the celebration of Easter every Sunday in the Christian congregations of the second century.[3] Eventually these weekly commemorations appear to have melded into one annual Easter celebration. Early Church father Irenaeus documented this annual celebration as he wrote against the dogmatic position of Bishop Victor of Rome, who demanded that Easter be affixed to only one day (Irenaeus favored a date that coincided with the Jewish Passover). The fallout from that exchange confirms that by about AD 160 the Christian community had adopted a single, annual celebration.[4] The Christian community, however, was far from unified concerning the date of Easter.

In the second and third centuries, controversies surfaced over which day of the week and which calendar to prefer for situating the Easter observance. In Rome the first Sunday after Nisan 14 (Passover) became the Christian feast of Easter. Others opted for a stronger paschal connection and insisted on the Jewish Passover as the exact date (these people were called "Quartodecimans"). And finally those in Syria and Mesopotamia insisted on following the spring equinox upon which the Jewish Passover was calculated, thereby removing the need to base Easter on the annual Jewish announcement of the date of Passover. The Council

## "The Christian History & Development of Easter"

of Nicea ostensibly settled the controversy when it decreed in AD 325 that Easter would be on the first Sunday after the paschal moon, which could not precede the vernal equinox. In practical terms this meant that Easter Sunday could fall on any one of the thirty-six days between March 21 and April 25.[5]

Overlooked in this fiat was a decision about which calendar would be the standard. Alexandria and the eastern churches chose the Julian calendar, while western Christians selected the Gregorian calendar. These differences have persisted for thousands of years and account for the modern discrepancies between eastern and western Christian dates for Easter.

During the first few centuries of early Christianity, the term *Easter* did not yet exist. Early Christians referred to Easter simply as *Pascha*, the Greek term for the Hebrew word *pesach*, or passover. In Latin and Romance languages the word for Easter is still a derivation of the Hebrew word *pesach*. In the English and Germanic cultures, the earliest mention of the word *Easter* comes from the English historian Saint Bede the Venerable. Writing in the eighth century, Bede claimed the term *Easter* referred originally to a pagan holiday centered on the Anglo-Saxon goddess Eostre, celebrating both spring and fertility. He buttressed his account by citing a provocative letter from Pope Gregory I. In this letter the pontiff suggested that missionary work among the heathens would improve if pagan holidays were synchronized with Christian celebrations. These assertions lead to the widespread conclusion that the Christian holiday Easter had its origins in a pagan fertility rite.[6]

## Celebrating Easter

In recent years a number of alternative explanations to the pagan theory have arisen. Among them is the notion that Easter is the abbreviated form of the German word for resurrection, *auferstehung*. Still another explanation is that the early Church referred to Easter week as "white week" because the newly baptized members dressed in white clothes. The plural of "white week" was very similar to the Old German word for dawn, *Eostarum*. When this was translated into English, it became the word *Easter*. While the etymology of the English term *Easter* remains uncertain, we have evidence that the annual Christian festival was firmly established by the second century.[7]

### CHRISTIAN EASTER TRADITIONS

The early establishment of Easter as the foremost Christian celebration facilitated almost two thousand years of religious traditions and rituals. Many of these practices developed from theological or liturgical moorings, while others emerged from a purely cultural context. Additionally, the Orthodox, Roman, and Protestant branches of Christianity heavily influenced the emerging traditions of Easter. From the onset, Easter became the center of the Christian calendar year. As a result, there were traditions to mark Easter both before and after this special event. Forty days before this holiday, a period of fasting and penitence was instituted as early as the fourth century. Known as Lent, this period was intended to purify the believer before the actual celebration of Easter and to serve as a reminder of the Savior's forty-day fast in the wilderness. Following Easter, a fifty-day period of celebration known

"THE CHRISTIAN HISTORY & DEVELOPMENT OF EASTER"

as Eastertide commenced and concluded with Pentecost.[8] In all, ninety days of the calendar year either anticipated or reminded the believers of this important day.

Christian churches today usually begin the Lenten period of fasting with a celebration called Ash Wednesday. Ashes are placed on the forehead of believers to symbolize penitence. Fasting has often given way to various forms of self-denial during these five weeks. The last week of Lent is called Holy Week.

The Sunday before Easter commemorates Jesus's triumphal return to Jerusalem before the Passover, known as Palm Sunday; many churches today reenact His triumphal entry by bringing palm fronds to their services. Four days later many Christians observe Maundy Thursday, also called Holy Thursday. This remembrance recalls the evening of the Last Supper and particularly emphasizes the washing of the disciples' feet. It was at that ancient event that Jesus commanded His Apostles to serve one another. The term *maundy* means "mandate" or "commandment."

For modern Christians, the Friday before Easter is the most important pre-Easter event. Known as Good Friday, this day highlights the Crucifixion of Jesus Christ. Generally, there is a worship service at midday followed by a period of fasting and contemplation. Orthodox churches and many Spanish-speaking countries reenact the procession of the cross. Often these same communities designate Good Friday as a public holiday. The day before Easter Sunday is called Holy Saturday. On this day Catholics commemorate Jesus's death in the tomb with a worship service known as the Great Vigil, or watch. The gathering occurs after nightfall and contrasts candlelight with darkness to symbolize the darkness of Jesus's death and the great light of His Resurrection. The service generally follows a precise schedule so that as midnight strikes, all the candles are lit from one great paschal candle. As was the custom from early times, modern Great Vigil services often include new baptisms and the dressing of cleansed individuals in white clothing. After the Easter mass, the service concludes with exultant music and celebrations.[9] A common Easter greeting is then shared with fellow worshippers—"Christ is risen!"—to which the greeted individual responds, "He is risen indeed!"

For Catholics, Easter culminates Sunday night at midnight. However, for Protestants, Easter means Sunday morning services. Many of these begin before sunrise on a hilltop and reenact the New Testament narratives of the empty tomb and the appearances of the resurrected Lord. Protestants have generally been more conservative in their Easter celebrations. While wide variations of Easter celebrations exist, Protestants with Puritan roots generally favor very modest expressions. On the other hand, the Civil War actually elevated Easter Sunday among American Protestants because it became customary to remember the casualties on this day.[10] In modern times, Easter commemorations have assumed an interdenominational nature.

## POPULAR EASTER CUSTOMS AND SYMBOLS

Many of the popular Easter customs have become a blend of the sacred remembrances of Christ's Resurrection and the secular celebrations of spring. Some of the more

## "The Christian History & Development of Easter"

prevalent religious symbols are the empty cross, the lamb, and the Easter egg. The empty cross often projects the Protestant view that Jesus rose from His death; it symbolizes His ultimate victory. The lamb ties most Christians to both the Passover symbolism of the Paschal Lamb and the New Testament appellation of Jesus as the "Lamb of God" (John 1:29). Some Christians eat lamb as a part of the Easter feast, while others hang up pictures of lambs or bake lamb-shaped cakes.

Perhaps the most universal symbol of modern Easter celebrations is the Easter egg. Disdained by some as a pagan perversion and enthroned by others as a symbol of new life, the Easter egg probably had much milder origins. During the ancient practice of Lent, eggs were one of the forbidden foods. So when Easter dawned and those proscriptions were lifted, early Christians greeted each other with an egg as a gift. By the thirteenth century, these eggs were colored and decorated; in imperial Russia the egg custom was elevated to include precious objects decorated like eggs and adorned with jewels. While other explanations abound, such as the egg symbolizing new life or the worship of spring, the Lent-fasting explanation is well documented and appears to have a historical footing.[11]

On the other side of the spectrum are those Easter symbols and customs with a definite secular flavor. Among these are the Easter bunny; Mardi Gras, or Shrove Tuesday; and Easter promenades. For many, the Easter bunny tops the list of secular and commercial Easter customs. As with most modern traditions, however, the Easter bunny probably did have legitimate Easter roots. One plausible explanation ties this practice to Protestants in nineteenth-century Europe. As a rejection of the Catholic practice of fasting and then giving eggs as gifts, Protestants supposedly created a rabbit that laid the eggs, decorated them, and hid them.[12] Shrove Tuesday, or "confession Tuesday" (Mardi Gras in French), stands as another example of a wandering tradition. To begin a forty-day period of fasting in preparation for Easter, Christians created a day to revel and party. The result was a very nonreligious week of revelry and licentiousness.

Finally, the Easter promenade has become a prominent walk on Easter Sunday to display the new clothes purchased especially for Easter. (The most pretentious of these is in New York City around the Fifth Avenue area.) Yet this custom too seems to have a religious heritage. In the early church, congregants baptized on Easter Sunday were dressed in new white clothes to symbolize their purity and rebirth. Quite likely this practice merged with the commercialism of modern times to surface in the purchase of new clothes for Easter and the desire to display them. In some European countries, "these promenades are led by a person holding a cross or an Easter candle."[13] So while many Easter traditions and customs seem far removed from Easter, most of them are a blend of religious traditions with modern culture. It is amazing how diverse Easter traditions have become. But considering their two thousand years of historical development, perhaps these traditions demonstrate the deep need for devout Christians everywhere to remember the miracle of the Resurrection.

# "The Christian History & Development of Easter"

## Latter-Day Saint Easter Traditions and Attitudes

The Church of Jesus Christ of Latter-day Saints does not have a two-thousand-year tradition of Easter celebrations. Restored in 1830, the Church is unique in many of its traditions and celebrations. Nonetheless, the Church places great doctrinal emphasis on the miracle of the Resurrection and the importance of Easter.[14] What are the attitudes and traditions of faithful Latter-day Saints concerning Easter?

To ascertain the attitudes of Latter-day Saints, an informal survey was recently given to 404 active members in five different wards (local units) and two Brigham Young University classes. The survey consisted of fifteen questions and bore the broad title "LDS Holiday Survey" to avoid predisposing the participants toward Easter. It was administered three to five weeks before Easter Sunday. The results identified some interesting attitudes and trends among Church members. For discussion purposes, seven of the more relevant questions will be highlighted here (see the appendix for the complete survey).

One of the first issues that the survey tackled was in question 3. It asked the Latter-day Saint respondents to rank four major holidays in order of their "importance to you and your family today." The choices were Christmas, Easter, the Fourth of July, and Thanksgiving. The term "importance" was not further defined or nuanced. Christmas gained an expected 1.2 average rank (1 was most important, 4 was least important). Thanksgiving came in second with 2.4, Easter tallied third with 2.8, and Fourth of July came in last with 3.6. The remarkable result here was that Thanksgiving outpaced Easter by a substantial margin.

Question 4 was, "How far in advance do you begin preparations for [these] holidays?" Because of some extreme answers the median answer was computed for this question. Once again, the order of preparation time spent followed the same order the holidays were ranked. The largest preparation value was for Christmas at thirty days in advance of the holiday, followed by Thanksgiving at seven days, Easter at four days, and finally the Fourth at two days. The most interesting contrast here appears to be between Christmas and Easter. For most members, Christmas begins well before Thanksgiving has even been celebrated, while the Easter season begins in earnest only four days before the event.

Question 5 asked the respondents if they knew when the date of Easter was for this year. Again, the survey was administered three to five weeks before the holiday. Forty-four percent claimed that they knew the date for Easter, while 56 percent did not. Keep in mind that a number of these members were giving their answers within three weeks of Easter Sunday. Also, the percentages might have been substantially higher on the side of ignorance if the question had required the actual date rather than a simple "yes" or "no" answer.

The final four relevant questions moved from general recognition to specific traditions and practices. Question 7 asked, "Did you read from the scriptures the Christmas [or Easter] story this past year?" During Christmas, 81 percent read scriptures. However, only 41 percent said they did for

Easter. This means that almost 60 percent of these active Latter-day Saints did not read the Resurrection story during the Easter celebration. Question 10 asked how much time was spent reading the scriptures during the holidays. The median value was thirty minutes for Christmas and twenty minutes for Easter. Answers to these questions indicate that Easter scripture reading occurs in only a minority of Latter-day Saint homes and that the total time spent doing so is rather abbreviated.

The final two content questions examined the extent to which Church members engage in pre-Easter traditions. The five pre-Easter events mentioned in these two questions were the Triumphal Entry, Passover, Trial of Jesus, Crucifixion, and Resurrection. The first question looked at the five events in a ward context, and the second looked at them in a home setting: "Which of the following [five pre-Easter events] was discussed in your ward this past Easter?" and "Which of the following did you discuss (or review) in your home?" Concerning the Triumphal Entry, 8 percent discussed it with their ward, whereas 6 percent discussed it with their family. Concerning the Passover, 15 percent discussed it with their ward, while only 11 percent mentioned it at home. As expected, the highest participation came with the Resurrection itself, where 35 percent discussed it with their ward and 36 percent talked about it at home. The trend here was fairly consistent: the more time between the pre-Easter event and Easter morning, the less attention it received among Church numbers. Likewise, discussion of pre-Easter events (excluding the Resurrection) received less attention at home than at church. The overall observation from these two questions is that the Church members place little emphasis on traditional pre-Easter activities.

In conclusion, these seven questions posed to approximately four hundred Latter-day Saints revealed that the Easter celebration comes behind both Christmas and Thanksgiving in intensity. Ninety percent of these faithful members indicated Christmas was most important, while only 2 percent marked Easter as most important. Members also spend less time, only four days, in preparation for Easter, less than both Christmas and Thanksgiving. Fewer than half read the Easter story at home or knew when Easter was this calendar year. Finally, only one in six discussed or reviewed the events of the Passion week. Only one in nineteen discussed the Triumphal Entry. These participants sent a consistent message from their candid answers: the celebration of Easter among the Latter-day Saints receives little attention beyond a regular Sunday worship service.

## IMPLICATIONS AND OBSERVATIONS OF EASTER TRENDS AMONG LATTER-DAY SAINTS

These numbers and attitudes seem to misrepresent the doctrinal position of the Church. Did not President Hinckley unabashedly proclaim Easter as the greatest day, event, and miracle in all of human history? How, then, can we as Latter-day Saints project such incongruity between our doctrine and our practices? Perhaps the answers to these questions emanate from our religious position as a nontraditional Christian church.

# "The Christian History & Development of Easter"

The Church of Jesus Christ of Latter-day Saints was restored near Rochester, New York, in 1830. This founding was not a reformation or a modification of Christianity. It occurred during the religious fervor known as the Second Great Awakening in an area that was dubbed "the burned-over district." While the New York environment was decidedly Protestant, Mormonism embodied a more biblical Christianity and distanced itself from both Protestants and Catholics. Jan Shipps, a respected historian, has referred to Mormonism and its "otherness" in Christianity.[15] Inherent doctrinal differences meant that Mormons revered modern prophets, expanded the traditional canon, adhered to a strict health code, and worshipped in both temples and churches. These doctrinal differences included cultural differences as well. Avoiding the use of the cross, eschewing memorized prayers, building close communities, and espousing conservative values were just a few of the cultural patterns that emerged. These attitudes and differences appear to have substantially shaped the celebration of Easter among Latter-day Saints.

Traditional Easter celebrations usually begin with religious observances of Shrove Tuesday followed by Ash Wednesday and then Lent. A month or so later, these celebrations crescendo with Palm Sunday, Maundy Thursday, Good Friday, Holy Saturday, and finally Easter Sunday. During these events, Catholics and Protestants celebrate Mardi Gras, fast from certain foods, wave palm branches, attend special weekday services, and hold sunrise services—all in anticipation of Easter. Members of the Church celebrate in a much more subdued manner. Why? Is it because such celebrations are not biblically based? No, traditions such as Palm Sunday, Maundy Thursday, Good Friday, and Sunrise Sunday all have strong scriptural precedents. The reason appears to be grounded in the Latter-day Saint culture of "otherness."

All Christians struggle with pinpointing the yearly date of Easter, but many have help in the traditional pre-Easter events. For traditional Christians, the larger culture continues to remind them of Easter through events such as Mardi Gras, Lent, and Palm Sunday. Weeks, if not months before Easter, traditional Christians are reminded of its advent. Mormons who eschew these pre-Easter traditions forego these systemic reminders and are left on their own to remember Easter Sunday.

A final consideration about the Latter-day Saints' observance of Easter is the annual general conference held during the first weekend of April. For all devout Latter-day Saints, this event is as important as the State of the Union Address is for conscientious Americans. For two days the First Presidency, the Quorum of Twelve Apostles, and other high-ranking leaders address the Church on important and timely topics. General conference is a megaphone for Church counsel, and it often falls either on or around Easter Sunday. Because it calls out to every active Latter-day Saint, general conference inherently overshadows Easter and its traditions. Sometimes Easter occurs on the same day as general conference, and sometimes it falls on a regular Sunday. Combined with the difficulty of dating Easter and the desire for distinctiveness from traditional Christianity, celebrating this holiday is certainly laced with challenges for the Latter-day Saint community.

This understanding of Latter-day Saint culture does not necessarily mitigate or ameliorate the Easter discontinuity.

"The Christian History & Development of Easter"

Three times during a span of twelve years President Hinckley stressed the singular nature of this Easter miracle. His pronouncement appears intent on raising the importance of Easter and the miraculous Resurrection among Latter-day Saints. It is clear that a church with the fullness of the everlasting gospel must be centered on the miracle of the risen Christ. He emphatically concluded one of his recent Resurrection talks with the words, "Of all the events . . . of humanity, none is of such consequence as this."[16] It seems reasonable, then, that the central holiday of all Christianity should certainly be central in the lives of the Latter-day Saints.

## NOTES

1. Gordon B. Hinckley, "The Greatest Miracle in Human History," *Ensign*, May 1994, 72; "This Glorious Easter Morn," *Ensign*, May 1996, 66; "He Is Not Here, but Is Risen," *Ensign*, May 1999, 70.
2. The careful reader of the King James Version of the book of Acts might rightfully note that there is a passage which refers to "Easter" in the days of the Apostles (Acts 12:4). It should be understood, however, that this reflected a subjective interpretation on the part of the KJV translators. The standard Greek texts of this New Testament passage use the term *paschach* which all translate as *passover* (see *The Complete Parallel Bible* [New York: Oxford University Press, 1993], 2932–33).
3. See Alexander Roberts and James Donaldson, eds., *Ante-Nicene Fathers: Translations of the Writings of the Fathers down to AD 325*, vol. 1, *The Apostolic Fathers with Justin*

*Martyr and Irenaeus* (Grand Rapids, MI: Eerdmans, 1953), 186.
4. See Henry Chadwick, *The Early Church*, rev. ed. (London: Penguin Books, 1993), 84–85. For the dating of Easter, see F. L. Cross, *The Oxford Dictionary of the Christian Church* (Oxford: Oxford University Press, 1997), 522.
5. See Chadwick, *The Early Church*, 85.
6. See Bertram Colgrave and R. A. B. Mynors, eds., *Bede's Ecclesiastical History of the English People* (London: Oxford University Press, 1969), 107–9.
7. See *Encyclopedia Americana* (Danbury, CT: Scholastic, 2005), s.v. "Easter."
8. See *Encyclopedia Americana*, s.v. "Easter"; *New World Encyclopedia* (Funk & Wagnall, 2002), s.v. "Lent."
9. See *Encyclopedia Brittanica*, 15th ed., s.v. "Easter"; *World Book Encyclopedia*, 2006 ed., s.v. "Easter."
10. See *Encyclopedia Americana*, s.v. "Easter."
11. See *Encyclopedia Brittanica*, s.v. "Easter"; *Encyclopedia Americana*, s.v. "Easter."
12. See *Encyclopedia Brittanica*, s.v. "Easter"; *Encyclopedia Americana*, s.v. "Easter."
13. *World Book Encyclopedia*, s.v. "Easter."
14. See Hinckley, "The Greatest Miracle in Human History," 72–74; "This Glorious Easter Morn," 65–67; "He Is Not Here, but Is Risen," 70–72.
15. Jan Shipps, "Difference and Otherness: Mormonism and the American Religious Mainstream," in *Minority Faiths and the American Protestant Mainstream*, ed. Jonathan D. Sarna (Urbana: University of Illinois Press, 1998), 100–101.
16. Hinckley, "This Glorious Easter Morn," 67.

"The Christian History & Development of Easter"

# Appendix

## LDS Holiday Questionnaire
## N = 404

1. Were you raised LDS?

　　＿＿＿ yes　　　＿＿＿ no

2. Rank each of the following holidays (from 1 to 4) in order of their importance to you and your family **when you were a child** (1 being *most* important and 4 being *least* important).

　　Fourth of July　3.6　　　Christmas　1.1
　　Thanksgiving　2.5　　　Easter　　2.9

3. Rank each of the following holidays in order of their importance to you and your family **today** (1 being *most* important and 4 being *least* important).

　　Fourth of July　3.6　　　Christmas　1.2
　　Thanksgiving　2.4　　　Easter　　2.8

4. How far **in advance** do you begin preparations for the following holidays (not including meal planning and preparing)? **(median values)**

　　Fourth of July　**2 days**　　Christmas　**30 days**
　　Thanksgiving　**7 days**　　Easter　　**4 days**

CELEBRATING EASTER

5. Do you know what day and month Easter falls on this year?
    Yes   44%                  No   56%

6. Which of the following holidays were discussed in talks or lessons at **church** last year?
    Fourth of July   17%        Christmas   29%
    Thanksgiving   25%         Easter   29%

7. Last year at home did you:
    Read the Christmas story from the scriptures?
      Yes   81%                No   19%
    Read the Easter story from the scriptures?
      Yes   41%                No   59%

8. How does celebrating **Thanksgiving** help your **family** the most? (choose just one)
    ___ increases gratitude     ___ improves family unity
    ___ deepens spirituality     ___ other

9. Last year what percent of your family holiday celebrations (outside of church) was spent on religious versus nonreligious traditions? For example: 95% nonreligious + 5% religious (or) 50% nonreligious + 50% religious, etc.

**Fourth of July**
    ___% nonreligious traditions  ___% religious traditions
        (fireworks, picnics)      (scriptures, inspiring talks)

**Thanksgiving**
    ___% nonreligious traditions  ___% religious traditions
        (football, parades)

## "The Christian History & Development of Easter"

**Christmas**
   ___% nonreligious traditions ___% religious traditions
      (gift shopping, tree)

**Easter**
   ___% nonreligious traditions ___% religious traditions
      (eggs, clothing, food)

10. Last year approximately how much **time** did you spend at **home** discussing the **scriptures** on: **(median values)**

| | |
|---|---|
| Thanksgiving | 10 minutes |
| Christmas | 30 minutes |
| Easter | 20 minutes |

11. In the past did your family reenact the Christmas story?
   _____ yes       _____ no

12. Which of the following was discussed in your **ward** last year during **Easter** time?

| | | | |
|---|---|---|---|
| The Triumphal Entry | 8% | Crucifixion | 28% |
| Passover | 15% | Resurrection | 35% |
| The Trial of Jesus | 14% | none of the above | 0% |

13. Which of the following did you discuss (or review) in your **home** last year during **Easter** time?

| | | | |
|---|---|---|---|
| The Triumphal Entry | 5% | Crucifixion | 26% |
| Passover | 11% | Resurrection | 36% |
| The Trial of Jesus | 14% | none of the above | 8% |

RICK B. JORGENSEN

## Teaching the Doctrine of the Resurrection When Sharing the Gospel

During the Easter season, Christians around the world turn their thoughts and their hearts to Jesus Christ as they commemorate the last week of His life. Some Latter-day Saints wonder how best to celebrate this important religious holiday, unable to make the distinction between the traditions of other Christian faiths and scriptural truths associated with Easter. As a result, they may focus much of their attention on Christ's Resurrection but keep their thoughts and praise during the Easter season confined to subdued expressions in private environments. Easter is a celebration of the risen Lord, and Latter-day Saints should lead out in their celebration of this important

---

Rick B. Jorgensen is an instructor for the Church Educational System and teaches Church history and doctrine part time at Brigham Young University.

holiday, declaring the light and truth of the Restoration that promises the resurrection of all mankind.

As a seminary teacher in a small agricultural community, I wore a suit and tie, which sometimes led to questions about the nature of my work. On one occasion a Hispanic man who was interested in purchasing my van flagged me down on the road. He asked what I did for work. He was surprised that Latter-day Saints taught scriptures to high school students during the school day. He excitedly told me he was the new co-pastor for a local Christian church with a contingent Spanish congregation. This polite exchange led to a conversation about the basic doctrines of each other's faith. I asked about his belief in the Resurrection. Mistakenly thinking I was referring to the Second Coming, he slapped his chest, saying, "Él viene, mi amigo!" or "He is coming, my friend!" I asked him again his beliefs about the Resurrection, and he did not seem to understand what I meant. I asked if he believed that after Jesus was crucified He arose from the tomb with His physical body. He looked at me carefully and asked what I believed. After explaining the Resurrection of Jesus Christ, I testified of our eventual resurrection. He said simply and humbly, "That is what I believe."

Elder Jeffrey R. Holland taught, "When you declare the truth, it will bring an echo, a memory, even if it is an unconscious memory to the investigator, that they have heard this truth before—and of course they have."[1] Since missionary work is the business of spreading the good news of truth, my experience with that man impressed upon me the importance of teaching the doctrine of the Resurrection when sharing the gospel of Jesus Christ.

# "Teaching the Doctrine of the Resurrection"

## A Lack of Unity in Doctrine and Understanding

During the Savior's mortal life, the Jewish religious community was divided on the issue of resurrection. The New Testament states clearly that the Sadducees said there would be no resurrection (see Matthew 22:23; Acts 23:6–8). After the glorious Resurrection of Jesus Christ, there continued to be division among Christians concerning a physical resurrection. St. Augustine (circa AD 430), the first archbishop of Canterbury, wrote about this doctrine that has long split Christianity, "In nothing is there so much conflict and controversy among Christians themselves as on the subject of the resurrection of the flesh."[2] The controversy of which St. Augustine spoke appears to be centered on the idea of a literal, corporeal resurrection.

Kenneth Woodward wrote in his featured *Newsweek* article entitled "Rethinking the Resurrection" that even though "most Christians still believe in the Risen Jesus . . . very few Christians are literalists on this point, and . . . there is a range of opinion on what the Resurrection means."[3] Divergent doctrinal opinions have historically fueled Protestant offshoots and continue to be a catalyst for change. The result is the present diversity in Christian doctrines, including that of a physical resurrection.

A poll by the National Opinion Research Center asked Americans, "Will life after death be a spiritual life, involving our mind but not our body?" Seventy-five percent of respondents believed that would be the case.[4] Later the Gallup Organization polled 750 adults about resurrection, asking whether or not people will have "human form" in the life after death: 43 percent said yes, and the remaining 57 percent disagreed or did not know.[5] According to this poll, the majority questioned did not know or did not believe in a resurrection that includes human form. If resurrection is indeed a significant Christian doctrine, then these results demonstrate a need for clarification of this truth. Although the poll data is now around twenty years old, the responses indicate that the reality of a physical resurrection confuses many Americans, though many do still believe in a corporeal resurrection.

These poll questions hint at the disparity between what resurrection is and what the general population understands it to be. The division in doctrinal understanding concerning resurrection raises the question, "What effect does an understanding of the doctrine of the Resurrection have upon religious observance in general as well as on human behavior?" The idea that true doctrine correctly understood affects behavior could be significant in relationship to the doctrine of the Resurrection.[6] Christians and non-Christians might have a changed outlook if they were truly converted to the reality of the doctrine of the Resurrection. A true understanding of the Resurrection gives an eternal perspective for the physical body. The knowledge that not only the mind and spirit continue but that the physical body does as well changes the way humans treat their bodies and the way they think about the opportunity to progress in the eternities. Acceptance of Christ's physical Resurrection strengthens belief in the eternal nature of humankind.

# "Teaching the Doctrine of the Resurrection"

## Resurrection in the Old Testament

The word *resurrection* appears 124 times in the standard works of The Church of Jesus Christ of Latter-day Saints, in sixty-two different passages. Comparing this to the word *baptism*, which is referenced in forty-two passages, illustrates the prevalence of *resurrection* in the scriptures. Like the word *baptism*, the word *resurrection* is not specifically used in the Old Testament, though latter-day scripture confirms that ancient prophets spoke of resurrection during the Old Testament era. Moses 7:62 reads, "And righteousness will I send down out of heaven; and truth will I send forth out of the earth, to bear testimony of mine Only Begotten; his resurrection from the dead; yea, and also the resurrection of all men."

Old Testament references to resurrection—without using the actual word—add great insight to our understanding of this doctrine and confirm that the prophets of old indeed looked forward to a glorious resurrection. The seemingly forsaken Job spoke on two separate occasions of his eventual resurrection. He specified a corporeal resurrection, claiming, "And though after my skin worms destroy this body, yet in my flesh shall I see God" (Job 19:26; see also Job 14:14). Snapshots of other references reveal the hope others had in their resurrection. In 1 Samuel 2:6 Hannah sings praises to the Lord, testifying of her conviction that the Lord brings about resurrection, saying, "The Lord killeth, and maketh alive: he bringeth down to the grave, and bringeth up." Isaiah prophesied that Christ would overcome death and be resurrected, thus opening the way for all men to be resurrected (see

Isaiah 25:8). The ancient prophet Ezekiel was carried away in vision by the Lord to a valley of dry bones, where he was shown the restoration of the house of Israel. In graphic detail, Ezekiel saw physical bodies arise when sinew, flesh, and skin were put back on the bones and breath returned to those slain (see Ezekiel 37). The book of Daniel prophesies of two resurrections, one unto eternal life and the other to shame and contempt (see Daniel 12:2). Hosea speaks for the Lord when he proclaims that He will ransom His people "from the power of the grave" (Hosea 13:14).

## RESURRECTION IN THE NEW TESTAMENT

Christ's victory over death and His compassion for those left to mourn are powerful elements in scripture. The New Testament describes three incidents where Christ raised someone from the dead. These were not permanent physical resurrections but restorations to mortal life. All three were raised as Christ demonstrated His compassion for those who suffered from the untimely deaths of loved ones. These events strengthened faith in His power over death and must have prepared the hearts of the people for His Resurrection. When Christ rose from the tomb, however, it was permanent. He was not merely raised from the dead but was resurrected, becoming "the firstfruits of them that slept" (1 Corinthians 15:20). Before raising His friend Lazarus from the dead, Christ comforted Martha, explaining that He is the Resurrection and the Life and that those who believe this shall live eternally both spiritually and physically (see John 11:17–27).

## "Teaching the Doctrine of the Resurrection"

The Resurrection of Christ is a pinnacle doctrine in the New Testament. In fact, it is central to the concluding chapters of all four Gospels. Luke offers a vivid account of the Lord's first appearance as a resurrected being to His Apostles. Although the doors had been shut, He appeared in the room, and those present had the privilege to touch and be touched by Him, as well as to see Him eat:

> And as they thus spake, Jesus himself stood in the midst of them, and saith unto them, Peace be unto you. But they were terrified and affrighted, and supposed that they had seen a spirit. And he said unto them, Why are ye troubled? and why do thoughts arise in your hearts? Behold my hands and my feet, that it is I myself: handle me, and see; for a spirit hath not flesh and bones, as ye see me have. And when he had thus spoken, he shewed them his hands and his feet. And while they yet believed not for joy, and wondered, he said unto them, Have ye here any meat? And they gave him a piece of a broiled fish, and of an honeycomb. And he took it, and did eat before them. (Luke 24:36–44)

The experience must have been life altering for those present and so incredible that Thomas doubted it until he personally witnessed the risen Lord. The effect of Christ's first appearance to His Apostles cannot be measured directly, but subsequent scriptural accounts describe converted Apostles who testified of the resurrected Christ even though they faced persecution. Christ had demonstrated His power over death by raising those aforementioned, but a resurrected, immortal being was almost unbelievable for even those closest to the Savior during His mortal ministry.

Special among the accounts of the resurrected Lord is His appearance to Mary Magdalene outside the tomb as recorded in John 20:

> But Mary stood without at the sepulchre weeping: and as she wept, she stooped down, and looked into the sepulchre,
>
> And seeth two angels in white sitting, the one at the head, and the other at the feet, where the body of Jesus had lain.
>
> And they say unto her, Woman, why weepest thou? She saith unto them, Because they have taken away my Lord, and I know not where they have laid him.
>
> And when she had thus said, she turned herself back, and saw Jesus standing, and knew not that it was Jesus.
>
> Jesus saith unto her, Woman, why weepest thou? whom seekest thou? She, supposing him to be the gardener, saith unto him, Sir, if thou have borne him hence, tell me where thou hast laid him, and I will take him away.
>
> Jesus saith unto her, Mary. She turned herself, and saith unto him, Rabboni; which is to say, Master. (John 20:11–16)

In the following verse, Christ commands Mary, saying, "Touch me not" (John 20:17). However, a more literal translation of this passage from Greek would read, "Stop holding on to me." The Joseph Smith Translation supports this interpretation, saying, "Hold me not,"

## "Teaching the Doctrine of the Resurrection"

thereby strengthening the proof that she witnessed a bodily resurrection as Mary could touch Christ's body. This very personal account of the resurrected Lord's appearance to Mary brings peace to those whose faith has been tested by the loss of a loved one. A witness of the resurrected Christ can bring comfort to friends, neighbors, and loved ones; it can also strengthen our faith in our own eventual resurrection.

Besides testifying of the Resurrection of Christ, the New Testament records that others were resurrected after He arose. Matthew 27:52 declares, "And the graves were opened; and many bodies of the saints which slept arose." This is an important passage, since it contradicts those who believe that the privilege of a physical resurrection was reserved for Christ only. According to John, Christ taught the Jews that sought His life that the Father was involved in the resurrection of all men and that Christ Himself was there to do the work of the Father (see John 5:17–21).

In the Acts of the Apostles, the role of the Apostles as testifiers of the Resurrection is paramount. As the Apostles sought the conversion of not only all Jews but of all men, their testimonies were centered on the risen Lord (see Acts 4:33). Their proclamations put their very lives in jeopardy. As the Apostles repeatedly testified that Jesus Christ the Son of God had been crucified but rose triumphantly from the grave, the Resurrection became the central message of nascent Christianity.

Jewish rejection of Christ's Resurrection led the Apostle Paul to turn his efforts toward the conversion of Gentiles (see Acts 13:45–48). Resurrection, which was so controversial for some, appears to have been central to Paul's message.

When Paul spoke in defense of his life before Felix, he took occasion to testify of the physical resurrection of the dead, both of the just and unjust (see Acts 24:15). Later, standing before King Agrippa, Paul asked why it was so incredible or unbelievable that God would raise the dead (see Acts 26:8). The Resurrection was foundational to Paul, and he testified of the resurrection of all humankind as he appeared before kings and magistrates.

Paul's epistles also contain powerful testimonies of resurrection. To the Romans, the Ephesians, the Philippians, and the Colossians, Paul testified that our mortal bodies would be quickened, or resurrected, to an immortal physical state (see Romans 8:11; Ephesians 2:5; Philippians 3:21; Colossians 2:13). Paul likewise understood and testified that there was an order to resurrection associated with righteousness and a belief in Christ. Paul continued to teach the reality of resurrection during his many years of missionary work as he encouraged all men and women to come unto Christ. To the Corinthians, Paul wrote: "But now is Christ risen from the dead, and become the firstfruits of them that slept. For since by man came death, by man came also the resurrection of the dead. For as in Adam all die, even so in Christ shall all be made alive. But every man in his own order: Christ the firstfruits; afterward they that are Christ's at his coming" (1 Corinthians 15:20–23).

Paul taught that personal righteousness affects not only being resurrected but also the order in which people would be resurrected. To the Thessalonians he wrote that those who die while following Christ will be resurrected first (see 1 Thessalonians 4:16). And his epistles do not stand alone among the New Testament texts in declaring this truth. In

## "Teaching the Doctrine of the Resurrection"

Revelation, John added his testimony of the importance of personal righteousness as it relates to physical resurrection. The faithful were promised the privilege of the First Resurrection. Peter's faith in Christ was strengthened by his hope in resurrection (see 1 Peter 1:3), and he recognized that the gift of resurrection saved him from physical death (see 1 Peter 3:21). Clearly the witness of the Resurrection was foundational to the testimony of Christ's Apostles and the early Christian Church as described in the New Testament.

### Resurrection in the Book of Mormon

President Ezra Taft Benson explained the powerful role the Book of Mormon has in proving resurrection: "The Book of Mormon is also the keystone of the doctrine of the Resurrection. As mentioned before, the Lord himself has stated that the Book of Mormon contains the 'fullness of the gospel of Jesus Christ' (D&C 20:9).... The Book of Mormon offers so much that broadens our understandings of the doctrines of salvation. Without it, much of what is taught in other scriptures would not be nearly so plain and precious."[7] The Book of Mormon records Jesus Christ's appearance in the Americas as the resurrected and immortal Son of God. The Book of Mormon clearly prophesies of the resurrection of all humankind, even detailing the actual restoration of flesh and bone with spirit.

Many ancient prophets in the Book of Mormon testified of a physical resurrection. Nearly six hundred years before the birth of Christ, Nephi saw in vision that after Christ was slain He would rise from the dead (see 1 Nephi 10:11).

Nephi explained that resurrection included both the body and the spirit and that every human being would become incorruptible and immortal, clothed with purity and the robe of righteousness (see 2 Nephi 9:12–14). Elder Jeffrey R. Holland clarified this passage of scripture, promising, "As a universal gift flowing from the atonement of Christ, the Resurrection will clothe with a permanent, perfected, restored body every spirit ever born into mortality."[8] The Book of Mormon prophets understood that bringing to pass the resurrection of the dead was a significant part of Christ's role (see 2 Nephi 2:8; Alma 33:22; Alma 40:3; Helaman 14:15; Mormon 7:6). The Book of Mormon clearly teaches the corporeal resurrection of all people (see Alma 11).

The "crowning event" in the Book of Mormon is the appearance of the resurrected Christ in the Americas to the righteous who awaited His coming (introduction to the Book of Mormon; see also 3 Nephi 11–27). Christ taught and testified to the people of the certainty of their own resurrection. So paramount is the witness for physical resurrection in the Book of Mormon that Moroni, the concluding author, devotes his last passage to his conviction that his own spirit and body would again reunite in the resurrection (see Moroni 10:34). The testimonies of these ancient prophets in the Americas is another testament of Jesus Christ, giving credibility to an actual physical resurrection.

The Book of Mormon outlines the advantages of a glorified, resurrected body over just a spirit body. It testifies of a complete corporeal resurrection in which not even a

## "Teaching the Doctrine of the Resurrection"

hair of the head will be lost (see Alma 11:42–46). President John Taylor explained, "It requires both body and spirit to make a perfect man, whether in time or eternity."[9] Not just any physical body but a perfected body reunited with its spirit in its perfect form (see Alma 11:43). President Joseph Fielding Smith said, "Deformities will be erased and in the resurrection will be made whole."[10] President Brigham Young promised, "Those who attain to the blessings of the first or celestial resurrection will be pure and holy, and perfect in body."[11] The idea of a perfect body restored to its whole and complete form is miraculous, particularly for those deprived of health or wholeness in mortality. President Spencer W. Kimball testified, "When the body is resurrected, . . . we will have our limbs and all our faculties."[12] These promised blessings give hope to those in a fallen world. As Latter-day Saints we have the obligation to lift up the hands that hang down and strengthen the feeble knees (see D&C 81:5). We can do this when teaching and testifying of a glorious resurrection as we share the gospel of Jesus Christ.

### A LATTER-DAY SAINT PERSPECTIVE

The Bible Dictionary in the Latter-day Saint edition of the King James Version describes resurrection as "the uniting of a spirit body with a body of flesh and bones, never again to be divided." In answer to the question "Is Christ to be the only resurrected being?" the Bible Dictionary further explains that all who have lived upon this earth will be resurrected because of Christ's victory over death. Its definition of resurrection culminates with the proclamation that to be resurrected with "a celestial, exalted body is the center point of hope in the gospel of Jesus Christ. The Resurrection of Jesus is the most glorious of all messages to mankind."[13]

President Howard W. Hunter powerfully addressed the doctrinal significance of Christ's Resurrection to Latter-day Saints: "The doctrine of the Resurrection is the single most fundamental and crucial doctrine in the Christian religion. It cannot be overemphasized, nor can it be disregarded. Without the Resurrection, the gospel of Jesus Christ becomes a litany of wise sayings and seemingly unexplainable miracles."[14]

President Hunter's remarks assign great importance to this crucial doctrine, especially in missionary situations. When sharing the gospel of Jesus Christ, citing this crucial doctrine as the centerpiece of our testimony may significantly change behavior and speed the conversion process.

Speaking of Christ's Resurrection, President Gordon B. Hinckley said: "This was not an ordinary thing. It was the greatest event in human history. I do not hesitate to say that."[15] As the greatest miracle in human history, the Resurrection deserves a prominent place among the doctrines that Latter-day Saints include when sharing the gospel of Jesus Christ with friends or neighbors. Broaching the subject of the "greatest event in human history" should not be unduly difficult and is absolutely necessary because it is indeed a "crucial doctrine."

In a recent general conference, President James E. Faust testified of the significance of resurrection in relation

## "Teaching the Doctrine of the Resurrection"

to the fulness of the restored gospel of Jesus Christ: "With [the Apostasy], priesthood keys were lost, and some precious doctrines of the Church organized by the Savior were changed. Among these . . . [that] all mankind will be resurrected through the Atonement of Christ, 'both the just and the unjust.'"[16] Understanding the Apostasy and its continued effect on Christian doctrines helps explain the general lack of understanding and minimizing of resurrection's importance. When Latter-day Saints recognize this loss of truth concerning resurrection and their ability to bless the lives of others with this knowledge, they can declare this doctrine of salvation with confidence.

A conviction of resurrection will strengthen an individual's understanding of the purpose of this life and help them face challenges common to mortality. Truly believing in resurrection could heal the hearts of a couple who has lost a young child in death. Knowledge of the restoration of the physical body in resurrection could change the perspective of someone physically challenged, permanently injured, or undeveloped. Possibly the most significant change a testimony of resurrection can bring is eternal perspective and purpose. This belief can change the way one views life and death and the way one treats the body. It gives meaning to this life and helps explain the potential humankind has in the afterlife. Believing in the Resurrection is more than a spiritual crutch for the mentally weak; it strengthens the reality of our eternal nature.

# Celebrating Easter

## Resurrection and the Restoration

Elder M. Russell Ballard of the Quorum of the Twelve Apostles taught that our testimony of the Restoration should emphasize the reality of the Resurrection: "Without the Restoration we would not have the blessings of priesthood ordinances that are valid in time and eternity. We would not know the conditions of repentance, nor would we understand the reality of the resurrection. . . . Our love for the Lord and appreciation for the Restoration of the gospel are all the motivation we need to share what gives us much joy and happiness. It is the most natural thing in the world for us to do, and yet far too many of us are hesitant to share our testimonies with others."[17] Since the bar for missionary work has been raised and the Church's efforts to share the gospel have been centered on the Restoration, the question of how significant teaching the Resurrection should be in our missionary efforts is an important one.

President Joseph F. Smith, sixth President of the Church, wrote: "The greatest event that has ever occurred in the world, since the resurrection of the Son of God from the tomb and his ascension on high, was the coming of the Father and of the Son to that boy Joseph Smith, to prepare the way for the laying of the foundation of his kingdom—not the kingdom of man—never more to cease nor to be overturned."[18] Restored to the gospel of Jesus Christ through the Prophet Joseph Smith is the message that the resurrected Christ stands at the head of The Church of Jesus Christ of Latter-day Saints. With the Book of Mormon as another witness of the resurrected Christ, the kingdom of God is established on earth to prepare the earth for the

## "Teaching the Doctrine of the Resurrection"

Second Coming of the Messiah. Above all, the doctrine of resurrection with the light of the Restoration gives hope to all mankind that resurrection is a reality and that God's whole work and glory is to bring to pass the immortality and eternal life of man (see Moses 1:39).

I do not know what became of the man with whom I spoke of Resurrection, but I hope that he maintained a belief and a hope in that doctrine. President James E. Faust explained what a testimony of a literal Resurrection of the Savior can do, saying, "The depth of our belief in the Resurrection and the Atonement of the Savior will . . . determine the measure of courage and purpose with which we meet life's challenges."[19] If indeed that man embraced the doctrine of the Resurrection and it became part of his testimony of the Savior, then it must have helped him in his pursuit of truth.

Considering all the things that have been written and spoken concerning the Resurrection, it seems important to end with the testimony of the Prophet Joseph Smith concerning the resurrected Christ. "And now, after the many testimonies which have been given of him, this is the testimony, last of all, which we give of him: That he lives!" (D&C 76:22). Let us follow the example of great missionaries in scripture and counsel from living prophets to reach out and share the doctrine of resurrection and the great truth of the Restoration with all who will listen.

### NOTES

1. Jeffrey R. Holland, "Missionary Work and the Atonement," *Ensign*, March 2001, 11.

2. Augustine, quoted in Hugh Nibley, *The World and the Prophets*, ed. John W. Welch, Gary P. Gillum, and Don E. Norton (Salt Lake City: Deseret Book, 1987), 159.
3. Kenneth L. Woodward, "Rethinking the Resurrection," in *Newsweek*, April 8, 1996, 62.
4. National Opinion Research Center Survey, July 1984, in LexisNexis Academic Database; http://web.lexis-nexis.com/universe/ (accessed November 7, 2006). Forty-six percent of respondents said a "spiritual life, involving our mind but not our body" was "very likely." Twenty-nine percent called it "somewhat likely."
5. Gallup Organization Survey, December 1988, in LexisNexis Academic Database (accessed November 7, 2006).
6. See Boyd K. Packer, "Little Children," *Ensign*, November 1986, 16–18.
7. Ezra T. Benson, "The Book of Mormon—Keystone of Our Religion," *Ensign*, November 1986, 5–6.
8. Jeffrey R. Holland, *Christ and the New Covenant: The Messianic Message of the Book of Mormon* (Salt Lake City: Deseret Book, 1997), 244.
9. John Taylor, quoted in Jay A. Parry and Donald W. Parry, eds., *Understanding Death and the Resurrection* (Salt Lake City: Deseret Book, 2003), 219.
10. Joseph Fielding Smith, quoted in Parry and Parry, *Understanding Death and the Resurrection*, 222.
11. Brigham Young, in *Journal of Discourses* (London: Latter-day Saints' Book Depot, 1854–86), 10:24.
12. Spencer W. Kimball, quoted in Parry and Parry, *Understanding Death and the Resurrection*, 221.
13. Bible Dictionary, "Resurrection," 761.

14. Howard W. Hunter, "An Apostle's Witness of the Resurrection," *Ensign*, May 1986, 15.
15. Gordon B. Hinckley, "He Is Not Here, but Is Risen," *Ensign*, May 1999, 70; see also an address delivered by President Hinckley on Easter Sunday, 1994, wherein he said, "Today is observed as the anniversary of the greatest miracle in human history" ("The Greatest Miracle in Human History," *Ensign*, May 1994, 72).
16. James E. Faust, "The Restoration of All Things," *Ensign*, May 2006, 61.
17. M. Russell Ballard, "Creating a Gospel-Sharing Home," *Ensign*, May 2006, 84.
18. Joseph F. Smith, *Gospel Doctrine*, 5th ed. (Salt Lake City: Deseret Book, 1939), 495.
19. James E. Faust, "Woman, Why Weepest Thou?" *Ensign*, November 1996, 52.

# Index

## A

Alma the Younger, 40, 53, 123–24
Amulek, 50
Ash Wednesday, ix, 209
Atonement of Jesus Christ:
    definition of, 44
    enables our return to God, 26
    includes pains of every kind, 36, 40, 123
    incomprehensibility of, 43, 49
    infinite nature of, 47–49
    involves shedding of blood, 27
    vicarious gift, 14
    ways to access, 52

## B

Ballard, M. Russell, 240
baptism, 54
Bateman, Merrill J., 125–26
Bede the Venerable, 207
Benedict XVI, 178
Benjamin, King, 5058
Benson, Ezra Taft, 235
blasphemy, 159
Bread of Life discourse, 87
Bread of the Presence, 96

## C

Caiaphas, 153
calendar:
    Gregorian, 207
    Jewish: viii, 206
    Julian, 207

Cook, Gene R., 127
covenants, 54
creeds, Christian, 6
Crucifixion, 8, 20, 191

**D**

Daniel, 230
David, 184
Davies, Douglas, 5
Death:
    physical, 48
    spiritual, 48
devil (accuser), 26
Donne, John, 20

**E**

Easter:
    and Passover, vii–viii, 137, 206–7
    early celebration of, vii, 205–8
    Latter-day Saint celebration of, x, 19, 201, 213–18, 221–23, 225
    origin of word, 208
    symbols, 211–12
    traditions, 208–12
    Sunday, 212
Eastertide, 208–9
Enoch, 183, 193

Enos, 21–22, 56–58
Eostre, 207
Eyring, Henry B., 50
Ezekiel, 230

**F**

faith in Christ, 34–35, 52–53
Faust, James E., 238–39, 241
forgiveness, 48, 56

**G**

Garden Tomb, 3–4
Gethsemane, 120–21, 190
Gibbons, Francis M., 36
Gifts of Spirit, 3, 9
God the Father:
    as judge, 26
    balances justice and mercy, 26
    unity with Son, 37
Good Friday, ix, 11, 209
Great Vigil, 210
Gregory I, 207

**H**

Haight, David B., 181
Harris, Martin, 121–22
Hinckley, Gordon B., 177, 179, 201, 219, 238

# Index

Holland, Jeffrey R., 123–24, 128, 226
Holy Ghost:
    cleansing power of, 58–59
    gift of, 54–55
    withdrawal of, 122, 193
Holy Saturday, 209
Holy Week, 11
Hosea, 144–45, 230
Hunter, Howard W., 238

I

Irenaeus, 206
Isaiah, 125, 184, 229

J

Jesus Christ:
    accusations against, 60–67
    advocate with Father, 23–27
    Alpha and Omega, 38
    Bread of Life, 92
    condescension of, 37
    Creator, 14, 38
    Crucifixion of, 8, 20, 191
    divine nature of, 50
    eldest brother, 26

Jesus Christ (cont.)
    experiential knowledge of, 117
    Firstborn, 35
    glory of, 35–36
    great high priest, 27–29
    Immanuel, 16
    intelligence of, 118
    intercessory prayers of, 6, 115, 190
    Jehovah, 37
    life and light, 39
    Messiah, 97
    ministry of, 8, 14
    miracles of, 90–91, 163–64, 168–71
    omniscience of, 117
    origins of, 8
    Passion of, 8
    prophesied mission of, 45, 202–3, 182
    prophet, priest, and king, 22
    Resurrection of, 8–9, 204–5
    sacramental imagery of, 100–103
    shepherd, 146–47
    suffering of, 36, 40, 120–21, 190
    testimony of, 12

Jesus Christ (cont.)
   transfigured, 181
   trial of, 157
   triumphal entry of, 187, 209
   unity with Father, 37
   wounds of, 191
Jewish views toward Jesus, 98–99, 162–67, 186, 188
John, Apostle, 235
Josephus, 168–69

K

Kimball, Spencer W., 237
knowledge, ways to gain, 113–17

L

Lactantius, 167
Last Supper, ix, 189
Latter-day Saints:
   worship of Christ, 7–9, 11–12, 201
   Easter practices of, x, 19, 213–16, 218, 221–23, 225
Lazarus, 164, 187, 203, 230
Lent, ix, 208–9, 211
"Living Christ, The," 13–16

Luke, 204, 206, 231
Luther, Martin, 178

M

magic, Jewish views of, 162–67
manna, 90, 92–95
Mardi Gras, 212
Martyr, Justin, 206
Mary Magdalene, 232–33
Matthew, 189
Maundy Thursday, ix, 209
Maxwell, Neal A., 118, 124, 126–27
McConkie, Bruce R., 49, 88, 104–5, 190
McKay, David O., 115–16
Milton, John, 30
miracles, 163
Moses:
   law of, 99–100
   symbol of Christ, 92–93

N

Nelson, Russell M., 120
Nephi, 128, 183, 186, 235
Nottingham, University of, 4–9

# INDEX

## O

obedience, 56–57

## P

Pace, Glenn L., 124–25
Palm Sunday, ix, 10, 209
Paschal Lamb, 101
*Pascha*, viii, 207
Passion Week, ix
Passover:
    and Bread of Life discourse, 89–90, 101
    and Easter, vii–viii, 137, 206–7
    Resurrection during, vii, 206
    Savior's last, 90, 137, 187
Paul, Apostle, 29, 119, 180, 185, 204–5, 233–34
Pentecost, ix
Peter, Apostle, 104, 167, 179, 185, 235
Pharisees:
    accusations of, 151
    and law of Moses, 139
    and Romans, 153
    and table fellowship, 143
    and temple worship, 141
    and tithing of food, 141, 150

Pharisees (cont.)
    and washing of hands, 148
    hostility of, 140, 152–53
    ritual purity of, 139, 141
    self-justification of, 145
    traditions of, 148, 150
Phelps, William W., 177
Pilate, Pontius, 165, 168
prayer, 56
Preston England Temple open house, 10–12
priesthood holders, foreordination of, 33–34
prophets, testimony of, 13–16, 45

## R

repentance, 53–54
Resurrection:
    American beliefs concerning, 227–28
    Book of Mormon doctrine of, 48, 235
    Jewish beliefs concerning, 227
    Latter-day Saint celebration of, x, 225
    Latter-day Saint doctrine of, 225

Resurrection (cont.)
    New Testament doctrine of, 230
    of Jesus Christ, ix, 8–9, 202–3
    Old Testament doctrine of, 229
    universality of, 237–38
Robinson, Stephen E., 122

**S**

sacrament, 14, 88, 100–103, 189, 206
Saduccees, 158
Sanhedrin, 158
scriptures, importance of, 55
Shipps, Jan, 217
Shrove Tuesday, ix, 212
Smith, Joseph, 12, 15, 36, 241
Smith, Joseph F., 240
Smith, Joseph Fielding, 180, 191, 237
Snow, Eliza R., 192
sorcery, 164

**T**

Talmage, James E., 49, 98, 181, 192

Tertullian, 206
testimony:
    gift of Spirit, 3
    keys to obtaining, 2–3, 17
    of apostles and prophets, 13–16, 45
    of Jesus Christ, 12
Thomas, Apostle, 231

**W**

Water of Life discourse, 96

**V**

Victor, Bishop, 206

**Y**

Young, Brigham, 120

**Z**

Zacharias, 188
Zechariah, 191
Zenos, 193